DEEP STATE DEFECTOR II

RAHUL
MANCHANDA

508 West 26th Street KEARNEY, NE 68848
402-819-3224
info@medialiteraryexcellence.com

CONTENTS

Deep State Shows They Control National Security with Michael Flynn Resignation

T he Deep State has at last revealed themselves to be even higher than the US National Security advisor and the president of the United States.

The Deep State does not ever want peace with Russia or a respite in their interventionist wars overseas.

They have thus far lobbed "softballs" at President Donald Trump, such as with their control over the mainstream media's relentless attacks on Donald Trump, his character, his nominee choices, his vision, his America-first policies, and other decisions that he has made.

The Deep State has also used their thoroughly corrupted judiciary at their disposal to thwart and sabotage Donald Trump's executive orders, with their corrupted judges stockpiled in the federal, state, and local courts for literally the past at least twenty-eight years, all the way from President George Herbert Walker Bush starting in 1988, to Bill Clinton, to George W. Bush, and then through Obama all the way until 2016.

The US Congressional and Senatorial gridlock established by the Deep State has also stood in Trump's way, but they were relatively easier to manage and move around for the Great Deal Maker (and Twitter communicator), Donald Trump.

However, now, with the latest revelation that General Michael Flynn, an ardent promoter of peace with Russia and the removal of sanctions, as well as nonintervention in other trouble spots throughout the world, the Deep State has literally pulled the proverbial rabbit out of the hat and have now fully revealed their hand, the question is, who exactly made this happen, and who were their handlers?

That person, whoever he is, has been revealed to be the ultimate emissary and messenger of the much-feared and shadowy American Deep State, someone who could force the resignation of one of the most powerful, sensitive, and highest security clearance positions within the executive branch of the United States.

Even former CIA Director James Clapper got a free pass by this Deep State when he, under full oath, openly and overtly *lied* to the entire United

States Congress and Senate when he stated that NSA surveillance was not comprehensive and was not listening in on each and every American citizen's phone calls, e-mails, faxes, and other communications, 24-7, 365 days a year.

This was a bald-faced and abject lie, as revealed by whistleblower Edward Snowden, and even worse, since it was under oath in front of the entire US Congress and Senate, it was complete and total *perjury*. This was not just an impeachable offense but one that can send you to jail for a thousand years.

Yet James Clapper was allowed to walk, given a free pass. Why?

Because James Clapper was a total stooge and errand boy for the American (and now Global) Deep State and did exactly what they told him to do whenever they told him to do it, even when his actions were antithetical to the interests of the American people or the rest of the people of the world.

This was his reward for faithfully carrying the Deep State's water.

Now, with the forced resignation of General Michael Flynn from his National Security advisor position, the message from the Deep State to President Donald Trump is crystal clear:

The Deep State is fully in control, fully in charge, and we can even casually throw out your most important and sensitive appointment in your cabinet and administration to date, so you better do exactly what we tell you to do whenever we tell you to do it and exactly in the manner that we prescribe.

Only a few weeks ago, in what is now obvious in hindsight, Michael Flynn, in a fit of feverish desperation to save his job, went off on a half-cocked rampage on live national television when he stated, "We are hereby putting Iran on notice!"

This was an obvious attempt to appease the most fringe elements of the Israeli government, but someone within the Deep State did not care about catering to the most extreme Israelis because the Deep State has other plans for Israel, Iran, and the rest of the Middle East, possibly World War III by and between purposefully created, cultivated, and funded radical Islam and radical Zionism, as predicted and described by Thirty-Third-Degree Freemason Albert Pike in the late 1800s?

Well, now with the forced ejection of the rational and reasonable peacemaker Michael Flynn, the prospect of World War III has become that much closer.

2

Does Donald Trump Have the Fortitude to Take On and Defeat the Deep State?

D onald Trump needs to study well how Vladimir Putin defeated the Deep State in order to liberate his people and his country from occupation.

With the recent headlines centering on the forced resignation of National Security advisor Michael Flynn, a rational voice of reason, peace with Russia, and an end or retrospection of stupid interventionist foreign wars (except his lashing out at Iran last week, which many believe was a last-ditch attempt to save his job by kowtowing to Neoconservative elements within the Deep State), as well as his moral clarity on exposing the etiology of ISIS as having been created, nurtured, funded, cultivated, and used by the global oligarchy/plutocracy to accomplish their goals of global chaos, clamping down on civil liberties, austerity programs, and other draconian, prison-planet end goals, it appears that the gauntlet has been thrown down by the anti-Trump elements within the Deep State Intelligence Community, forged over the past twenty-eight years, all the way from President George Herbert Walker Bush, through Bill Clinton, onward through George W. Bush, and then finally topped off by Barack Obama.

Even though Donald Trump's various America-first agendas were pronounced crystal clear since the day he began to run for office, he is now fully hitting the Deep State obstructionists on a near daily basis, who are literally using their clandestine skills to destroy his agenda and, consequently, the mandate given to him by the American people in the November 2016 election.

Like Vladimir Putin before him, upon taking office in 2000 from punch-drunk oligarch tool Boris Yeltsin, Donald Trump has inherited a deeply entrenched Deep State / Military Industrial Complex / National Security State / Intelligence Community / mainstream media oligarchy / plutocracy (but at least in the former USSR and Russia, the American

Neoconservatives/Neoliberals were openly called Communists).

But the mild-mannered, even-tempered, cool-as-a-cucumber Vladimir Putin, with his steely gray eyes, nonassuming, nonthreatening stature, and impeccable manners, literally dealt with his own Deep State Neocon obstructionists with the holy hellfire of one who was fiercely committed to rescuing his nation from the hellish bankruptcy, starvation, and destruction of the middle class from the pronounced oligarchy/plutocracy who was literally raping, pillaging, exploiting, and using the deeply impoverished and bullied Russian people, saving them from near-certain oblivion and subjugation.

For example, almost immediately after assuming office, Vladimir Putin, upon encountering the old, deeply entrenched, Deep State obstructionist, oligarch/plutocrat Communists within his own government, who tried to thwart and block his every move and policy decision designed to help his own Russian People, took on and defeated all his enemies one by one.

Donald Trump would be wise to follow his counsel and experience.

In order to "make America great again," it will be necessary to jail his Deep State obstructionists.

Americans want to fall in love with and take pride in their country again, as well as their leader.

Donald Trump was elected to be that leader because the American people believed that he had the balls and the smarts to beat these Deep State obstructionists and rout them out of the government—and this is no easy task.

He now needs to fight to keep it, for the sake of the American People that elected him, against the unelected Deep State, which is now showing signs of success in destroying him (and consequently the Great Hopes of Americans).

Blaming Immigrants for the American Police State

The oligarchs/plutocrats in America are only too happy when the American People falsely blame all of their societal, economic, and existential ills on immigrants (both illegal and legal) rather than where the blame rightfully belongs—at the feet of the oligarchs.

Watching the constant Fox News broadcasts around the clock, one would think that you were watching Nazi Germany in the showcasing of the abject hatred, vitriol, and scapegoating of an entire class of people for the ills and failings of the American police state in the modern age.

Throughout history, and especially during the last seventy years, immigrants and illegal aliens have always become the focal point for corrupted politicians who represent the shadowy oligarchs/ plutocrats in order to deflect the very real and reasonable anger of the citizenry to explain why there are no jobs, the reduced money in circulation, why living standards have decreased, why wages are depressed, and other societal ills that occur when the oligarchs/plutocrats have way too much power over the daily lives of the citizens that they rule over. If one were to watch a steady diet of Bill O'Reilly or Sean Hannity on Fox News, one would think that there is a direct correlation between illegal aliens and criminal activity.

They keep pointing to statistics and fancy graphics somehow linking illegal (or even legal) immigrants to criminal activity and convictions, when in fact these same news-talking heads of the mainstream media are deliberately hiding and obfuscating the hard fact that over seventy million American citizens (one-fourth of the country) have been convicted of a crime in the United States of America police state, especially since the 1994 enactment of the Joe Biden / Bill Clinton VCCLEA Law, which incarcerated 1/3 of all blacks, 1/6 of all Latinos, and 1/11 of all whites without probable cause, evidence, or due process in direct violation of the inalienable rights afforded by the US Constitution.

Seventy million Americans with criminal records in America—this is larger than the entire population of France.

So this is a major fallacy to attempt to link up illegal (or even legal) aliens/immigrants with criminal activity, convictions, or anything of the sort.

The absurdity of this illusion is even being used to push for a "special office" in the White House to provide "extra support" and "help" for American citizens who are victims of criminal activity by illegal aliens, but what about victims of crime by American citizens, which is nearly one hundred times higher?

Of course we will never see a special office in the White House for American-citizen victims of American-citizen crimes, because that would simply not complete, complement, or support the false narrative of the oligarchs/plutocrats that (mostly) brown illegal aliens somehow are raping and pillaging good, patriotic American (mostly) white people all across America, and you won't have the Hitlerian or Mussolini-like ability to blame the boogeyman for the societal, economic, spiritual, and existential ills being perpetrated by the oligarchs/plutocrats in America who are literally playing the proverbial fiddle while Rome burns and are more than happy for mainstream middle Americans to attack, burn, beat, abuse, harass, intimidate, and blame immigrants instead of turning their righteous indignation and anger against them, where it rightfully belongs, enabled by their political whores and lackeys in the US Congress and Senate, who are literally paid (lobbied) to aid and abet the oligarchs'/plutocrats' high crimes, treason, and misdemeanors.

The Deep State Oligarchs/Plutocrats Want to Keep America Drugged

T he oligarchy want to desperately keep America (and especially its youth) hopelessly drugged so that they never wake or rise to challenge their hegemonic status quo and world order.

As was predicted in Aldous Huxley's *Brave New World*, the elite have a vested interest in keeping their subjugated populace drugged to the maximum extent possible so that they do not ever wake from their stupor in order to challenge their soft (and sometimes overt) tyranny over them.

Brave New World is a novel written in 1931 by Aldous Huxley and published in 1932. Set in London in the year AD 2540 (632 AF—"After Ford"—in the book), the novel anticipates developments in reproductive technology, sleep-learning, psychological manipulation, and classical conditioning that combine profoundly to change society.

The World State was built upon the principles of Henry Ford's assembly line: mass production, homogeneity, predictability, and consumption of disposable consumer goods. While the World State lacks any supernatural-based religions, Ford himself is revered as the creator of their society, but not as a deity, and characters celebrate Ford Day and swear oaths by his name (e.g., "By Ford!"). In this sense, some fragments of traditional religion are present, such as Christian crosses, which had their tops cut off to be changed to a T.

From birth, members of every class are indoctrinated by recorded voices repeating slogans while they sleep (called hypnopædia in the book) to believe their own class is superior, but that the other classes perform needed functions. Any residual unhappiness is resolved by an antidepressant and hallucinogenic drug called soma.

This is why the oligarchy/plutocracy supports a vibrant pharmaceutical industry, consisting predominantly of antidepressants, antianxiety, and antihuman-emotion drugs.

As was explained in Zero Hedge's article by Michael Snyder in "The Drugging of America Summarized in 19 Mind-Altering Facts," the author makes the following points:

The American people are the most drugged people in the history of the planet ... Illegal drugs get most of the headlines, but the truth is that the number of Americans that are addicted to legal drugs is far greater than the number of Americans that are addicted to illegal drugs ... close to 70 percent of all Americans are currently on at least one prescription drug ... In addition, there are 60 million Americans that "abuse alcohol" and 22 million Americans that use illegal drugs ... What that means is that almost everyone that you meet is going to be on something. That sounds absolutely crazy but it is true ... We are literally being drugged out of our minds ... there are 70 million Americans that are taking 'mind-altering drugs' right now ... If it seems like most people cannot think clearly these days, it is because they can't ... We love our legal drugs and it is getting worse with each passing year ... And considering the fact that big corporations are making tens of billions of dollars peddling their drugs to the rest of us, don't expect things to change any time soon ...

The pharmaceutical industry funds with billions of dollars medical doctors and scientific whores who have categorically declared that the vast majority of Americans are bona fide "mentally ill" and thus require immediate, consistent, and long-term medication.

As was recited in the article "Psychiatrists: The Drug Pushers" published by the Guardian, "They say failed doctors become psychiatrists, and that failed psychiatrists specialize in drugs." The article asks the seminal question: "Is the current epidemic of depression and hyperactivity the result of disease-mongering by the psychiatric profession and big pharma? Does psychiatry have any credibility left at all?"

Unfortunately the long-term effects on the population are that the best and brightest, the ones who can easily gauge and determine just what exactly is wrong with the way the planet is being run, are oftentimes the most depressed, and therefore deemed to be mentally ill.

The *Psychiatric Times* issued an obviously well-hidden article by the oligarchs/plutocrats entitled "The Association between Major Mental Disorders and Geniuses," wherein the following was shown:

There exists an association between creativity and major mental disorders known since antiquity. The ancient Greeks considered both as "having been touched by the gods." Aristoteles, in his perspicacity, stated, "There is no genius without having a touch of madness." This phenomenon has been verified repeatedly in studies in the past. Does one phenomenon cause the other or do both share a common underlying factor or mechanism? How are geniuses able to accomplish "creative fits"? Although the proposed origin and mechanism of the brain function of creative geniuses is novel, empirical evidence is available to support this theory. Empirical evidence demonstrates that creativity and major mental disorders share a common pool made up of individuals with an extreme temperamental variant who, if endowed with other qualities (eg, high intelligence, tenacity, curiosity, energy) and live in a nurturing and complementary zeitgeist, can be creative geniuses. On the other hand, persons with a similar temperament but who do not have the additional qualities form a common pool of individuals who are at increased risk for a major mental disorder.

The early-on diagnosis and forced drug administration immediately silences and stifles creativity and problem-solving abilities, not to mention the motivation to undo the wrongs of the world, and renders the world's people leaderless.

The oligarchs'/plutocrats' favorite and most highly funded publications, such as the *Huffington Post*, eschew mercilessly and repeatedly that "early detection for mental illness is a must," while preaching on and on about today's young geniuses needing to be clipped right from the beginning before they do any real or meaningful damage to the existing status quo, which is often pretty evil.

These articles go on ad nauseam about how it is absolutely essential to take out these geniuses of society as early as possible, for the ultimate benefit of the ruling class.

And this is exactly what the oligarchs/plutocrats want.

Are Deep State Actors Trying to Frame Donald Trump with Hate Crimes?

I t's a bit strange (and very suspicious) that there has been a recent spate in hate crime incidents against visible minorities under the Trump administration.

It is interesting, to say the least, that there has been a recent spate of alleged hate crimes across America against visible minorities.

This makes no sense considering that Donald Trump has been very clear that he is an all-inclusive president and categorically rejects racism and discrimination in all its forms.

President Trump has reiterated repeatedly that he is "America first" and has appointed more of the supposed targeted minorities into his administration than any other president in American history, especially with regards to Indian Americans, so therefore this is all clearly a contrived operation by the hidden hand to further discredit Trump and delegitimize and undermine his presidency.

Now that the use of the mainstream media to target and undermine Trump has miserably failed, and the attempted coup d'état by claiming a Russian connection with most of Trump's high-level cabinet appointees is being exposed as more manufactured garbage, the Deep State is now getting more and more desperate.

And with regards to these "white racists" who are supposedly and "recently" targeting racial minorities, if they truly believed that Trump supported this nonsense, they would realize that they are actually doing a major disservice to their cause by engaging in conduct and behavior like this because it legally and morally undermines their entire movement and also would put them all under the federal, state, and local microscope, if not direct scrutiny from the president of the United States himself.

So to engage in such blatantly stupid behavior would actually hurt any legitimate white nationalist movement as it would most certainly result in their wholesale eradication like a crushed cockroach.

So who benefits from these targeted hate crimes all across the United States? One must once again the question, "Cui bono?" (Who benefits?)

Investigations need to take place on these hate crime assailants as to who their funding came from, who provided their training and weaponry, who controls them, who their handlers are, and who their connections are.

Additionally, the mainstream media needs to now also publish all alleged hate crimes that occurred under former presidents Obama, George W. Bush, Bill Clinton, and George H. Walker Bush, and why they were not really made into a big deal by the mainstream media when those Deep State presidents were at the helm.

Finally, the FBI needs to explain why hate crimes against Indian Americans were only started to be counted in 2013, literally only a few years ago, during the President Obama administration.

Was the Deep State prepping themselves to start keeping certain hate crime tallies targeted at certain ethnic and visible minorities only at that point, in late 2013, if, God forbid, one of their own was not elected president of the United States?

Inquiring minds want to know.

Donald Trump Needs to Pull a
Ronald Reagan and Start Firing All Disloyalists

D onald Trump needs to follow in the footsteps of his mentor Ronald Reagan and start pruning the tree of disloyalists within his government who are actively obstructing, sabotaging, and interfering with his Agenda for America.

Things are getting progressively worse for the Donald Trump administration as it seems that the Obama / Bush / Clinton / Bush Sr. holdovers of the past twenty-eight years are literally, and in almost coordinated unison, acting to team up and gang-stalk Donald Trump and his administration, cabinet appointees, and other Trump loyalists, using the mainstream media to carry their water.

But what did Ronald Reagan, one of Donald Trump's heroes, do when he was faced with insurgents within his own federal government?

One need only refer to the mass firings of belligerent, disloyal, and obstructionist air traffic control employees by Ronald Reagan in 1981 when they did not operate in the manner that he envisioned in his agenda for America.

The Professional Air Traffic Controllers Organization (PATCO) was a

United States trade union that operated from 1968 until its decertification in 1981 following a strike that was declared illegal and broken by the Reagan administration.

According to labor historian Joseph A. McCartin, the 1981 strike and defeat of PATCO was "one of the most important events in late twentieth century U.S. labor history."

In striking, the union violated 5 USC (Supp. III 1956) 118p (now 5 USC § 7311), which prohibits strikes by federal government employees.

Ronald Reagan declared the PATCO strike a "peril to national safety" and ordered them back to work under the terms of the Taft-Hartley Act.

Only 1,300 of the nearly 13,000 controllers returned to work.

Subsequently Ronald Reagan made the following statement to the media from the Rose Garden of the White House:

Let me read the solemn oath taken by each of these employees, a sworn affidavit, when they accepted their jobs: 'I am not participating in any strike against the Government of the United States or any agency thereof, and I will not so participate while an employee of the Government of the United States or any agency thereof.'

He then demanded those remaining on strike return to work within 48 hours; otherwise, their jobs would be forfeited.

On August 5, following the PATCO workers' refusal to return to work, Reagan fired the 11,345 striking air traffic controllers who had ignored the order and banned them from federal service for life.

They were replaced initially with nonparticipating controllers, supervisors, staff personnel, some nonrated personnel, and in some cases, by controllers transferred temporarily from other facilities.

Some military controllers were also used until replacements could be trained.

In 2003, Federal Reserve chairman Alan Greenspan, speaking on the legacy of Ronald Reagan, noted the following:

Perhaps the most important, and then highly controversial, domestic initiative was the firing of the air traffic controllers in August 1981. The President invoked the law that striking government employees forfeit their jobs, an action that unsettled those who cynically believed no President would ever uphold that law. President Reagan prevailed, as you know, but far more importantly his action gave weight to the legal right of private employers, previously not fully exercised, to use their own discretion to both hire and discharge workers.

President Reagan's director of the United States Office of Personnel Management at the time, Donald J. Devine, argued,

When the president said no … American business leaders were given a lesson in managerial leadership that they could not and did not ignore. Many private sector executives have told me that they were able to cut the fat from their organizations and adopt more competitive work practices because of what the government did in those days. I would not be surprised if these unseen effects of this private sector shakeout under the inspiration of the president were as profound in influencing the

13

recovery that occurred as the formal economic and fiscal programs.

In order of importance, Donald Trump needs to clean house in the following order, after testing the undying loyalty of these holdovers from previous administrations:

(1) The National Security Community,

(2) The Intelligence Community,

(3) The Military,

(4) The Federal Judiciary, and

(5) The White House Media Press Corps.

Cleaning house in the above five areas of federal government will very quickly have a pruning effect and allow Donald Trump and his staff to more easier carry out his agenda for America, unfettered, unsabotaged, and unobstructed.

Deep State Against Trump's Visa Ban Because Their False Flag Agents Are from Those Nations

President Donald Trump seeks to deny the Deep State oligarchs the pool from which they draw their false flag terrorists for their own nefarious purposes.

It is quite obvious why various elements of the Deep State are vehemently against President Donald Trump's temporary immigration ban and increased vetting procedures from certain countries in the world, and no, it's not because they are compassionate or even give a damn about these people.

This is obvious because these same Deep State elements in Europe and America actually caused this migrant crisis by their proxy bombing through NATO, ISIS, and Saudi Arabia of all these ravaged nations producing said migrants.

The reality is that this immediate but temporary shutdown of people streaming in as refugees or other types of immigrant and nonimmigrant visa holders from the temporarily banned nations are literally the pool or greatest cover from which various elements of the Deep State are able to easily recruit to commit these false flag terrorist attacks.

We have already seen this mechanism play out in Europe, with the various incidents as reported by Time magazine, namely the following:

(1) the string of ten stabbings in 2016,
(2) the Normandy church attack in July 2016,
(3) the Nice truck attack in July 2016,
(4) the Brussels bombings in March 2016, and
(5) the Paris attacks in November 2015.

This does not even begin to touch on the random attacks in the inevitable clash of civilizations"] being abruptly foisted upon Europe and America by these Deep State lunatics, who at the behest of the international bankers and corporations do not care how much violence takes place as long as they can work toward removing all borders, using the inevitable violence and terrorism that results to clamp down on everyone's civil liberties, human rights, and constitutional guarantees in order to solidify and consolidate their power.

15

President Donald Trump is not against immigrants or people traveling from those six nations temporarily banned and vetted further. He just wants to make sure that the Deep State doesn't get to keep recruiting from these pools to commit their terrorist attacks because he knows that these people are just being used by his fellow oligarchs/plutocrats to destroy the sovereignty and constitutional protections in the United States of America.

Remember that Trump is a former insider and knows exactly what these Deep State oligarch/plutocrat lunatics are up to, and he probably knows who they are, but has chosen to save the American republic from globalist destruction rather than remain in their ranks and watch the country he loves be destroyed.

If global integration is to take place, then it must be an organic, natural process, not one that is microwaved by these Deep State globalist sociopaths, who are all living comfortably in their gated communities, underground bunkers, or other safe enclaves, while watching from afar the cacophony and chaos resulting from their oligarch/plutocrat decisions, totally disconnected from reality and oblivious to the effects of their machinations.

Lucifer Found a New Home
How Russia and America Switched Places

The Luciferians, having been expelled from Russia after the fall of the Soviet Union, have encamped here in the United States of America.

Luciferian doctrine preaches that God has abandoned mankind— that we as humanity must take the place of this supposed God, who apparently has become something of an absentee landlord, that is, if he ever existed in the first place.

The founding fathers of the United States have been rumored to have been predominantly deists, which apparently means that although they acknowledged that the world was far too perfect and orderly to have been simply a fluke of the spark of accidental spontaneous creation and was created by some higher level of intelligence and origin, but that for some reason, no one was piloting the ship anymore and that it was up to humanity's betters to assume this governing role.

Enter the Freemasons and other secret societies that somehow believed that they were the chosen people who would navigate the ship of humanity toward its final shores, if not during the journey toward those shores.

But human beings are fallible, and we are daily confronted with our betters falling prey to all that humanity fails at—greed, avarice, sexual promiscuity, murder, rape, pillage, theft, deception, anger, hatred, destruction. In a nutshell, evil.

To that end, mankind's history has shown that human beings alone cannot be entrusted with humanity, and that if anything, our leaders need to have a full and final commitment to humility and an obeisance to a higher moral authority, one that can ensure that humanity lives and develops toward ultimate global peace and harmony, rather than death, destruction, enslavement, and cacophony.

Strangely, not much has been written about the seeming switching of places by and between Russia and America, the former of which went through nearly seventy years under Communist rule, starting in approximately 1917 as the USSR, run and led by Luciferians who believed that they knew better for humanity and who actively discouraged the belief in God or other forms of divine rule.

It should be noted that Luciferianism can quickly devolve into outright Satanism, or evil for the sake of evil itself, if those Luciferians begin to commit wanton acts of depravity against others in their pursuit of governance and control.

The Luciferian Communists billed themselves as realists and were not to be bothered with hocus-pocus notions of a man in the sky who issued his edicts and rules from the clouds above.

Contemporary comedians and political commentators who mock this concept of divinity abound in today's America.

But humanity witnessed that these enlightened men of Communism led that nation into a bona fide and draconian police state and, by the time that they were done, absconded with all that nation's wealth and power and became the oligarchs, leaving more than one hundred million men, women, and children dead in their wake, when their system of government finally and inevitably collapsed around 1989.

The necessity of their police state was justified by them, in that they believed that humanity needed to be controlled and culled as needed, as they believed that the masses were lawless and out of control, and since the rules of God were obsolete, that it was important to regulate and monitor everyone within their population.

This is why Vladimir Putin has emerged as a post-Communist leader and has reinjected the church back into the nation and is feverishly trying to bring the country back from the dead, and to a fairly large and successful extent, he has done so.

Meanwhile, the same Luciferians, in the forms of the international bankers, corporate CEOs, oligarchs, and plutocrats, have moved on after being expelled from Russia to focus on the United States and, to a lesser extent, Europe.

The second and third world remain largely their vassal states and would follow the example set by the strongest of the two different governing methodologies (Luciferianism versus Divinely Inspired Rule).

The problem with Luciferianism, however, as we have seen, is that it inevitably leads to the above-described societal ills, because, as a rule, mankind is hopelessly corruptible, and given enough money, military might, and power, will eventually succumb to human frailty and weakness, or madness, and kill off a great mass of innocent people in his paranoid and feverish attempts to more and more fully control the people that he rules over, all the while self-enriching himself at the expense of his governed people.

We have seen this in the former USSR, and we are now beginning to witness this same repeat of history in the United States, where the wealthy and powerful oligarchs/plutocrats have amassed greater and greater wealth and power, controlling the courts, the executive branch, and the legislature, while also holding the mainstream media in the palm of their hand.

The American police state continues to grow and grow in strength because the ruling class want more and more control over the masses and because they do not want to lose the advantages that they currently enjoy.

It is easy to see how this can quickly escalate and ignite into an explosion given the proper circumstances, such as a terror attack (false flag incentives for the oligarchs certainly abound, since they would be the primary beneficiaries of the consequent civil liberties and constitutional rights clampdown).

Therefore, it is vitally important that American leadership (public and private) learn from the lessons of history and not fall down the same path of the former USSR, or even Nazi Germany or Fascist Italy, which did not end well for either the oligarchs/plutocrats and their governed masses at all.

It is incumbent upon the ruling class to restore and replenish their faith, if not in the belief of a just and moral God, then their ultimate and total humility to a higher moral power, far greater than themselves.

Both their future, as well as the masses that they govern, depend upon it.

President Donald Trump Needs to Either Cancel, Repudiate, or Renegotiate the US Debt

P resident Donald Trump is the only man in history who can actually save the American people from global debt slavery by simply implementing what he has learned as a tough, seasoned New York City businessman.

The current US Debt hovers around twenty-three trillion dollars, and the overall debt is rumored to be around ten times that and is expected to grow by another ten trillion dollars in the next ten years.

It is absolutely and totally unpayable and has doomed the American people (and its government) to complete and total slavery.

The American people no longer have a government that answers to or works for them but rather takes their marching orders from the international central banks and, in the case of the United States, its incarnation as the Federal Reserve.

Born of a total fraud, a fraudulent inducement to contract foisted on the American people in December 1913, the bill enacting this financially extortionate and fiat currency banking system was literally rammed through Congress and the Senate during the Christmas festivities at that time, when 99 percent of the US Government was home for the holidays.

The legislation itself, which was drafted in secret by an ultra-secret financial banker cabal at the aptly named Jekyll Island, by men who literally used fake names in their transportation to get there, the entire process was a criminal conspiracy of the highest order.

This process alone would void and vitiate the US debt alone, because it is standard contract common law that one can void a contract by virtue of fraudulent inducement, misrepresentation, void for vagueness, nondisclosure, incapacity to contract, illegality, or for criminal purposes.

Past presidents Andrew Jackson and Thomas Jefferson fought viciously against central banking in the United States, opting instead for government-coined currency rather than farming it out to third-party interests, and certainly foreign ones at that.

They fought long, hard, and bloody wars, and in fact, many would argue that the United States itself was founded and declared independence from

England exactly because of the stranglehold the European Central Banks had over their originating country, but included the War for Independence of 1776, the War of 1812, and subsequently most major wars after that, all across the world, wherein the international bankers have commanded their host government country leaders to wage cruel, bloody wars against other nations who refused to host one of their international parasitic banks with which to exploit, drain, and extort their people with fractional reserve banking tactics and schemes.

Donald Trump is a seasoned and tough New York City businessman who has declared bankruptcy himself several times for his companies when he realized that it was no longer feasible, moral, or possible to pay bad or disputed debts. He also is no sucker and has a proven track record of telling bad debtors to go pound sand when they have presented him with invoices for faulty, substandard, shoddy, fraudulent, frivolous, illegal, or fictitious debt.

Therefore, he is exactly the man for this job, to tell the Federal Reserve and the international central bankers to take a long walk off a short pier.

The American people never consented to, or were informed fully or adequately, about the deal with the devil that is the Federal Reserve.

Had this vote been taken today, in the age of the internet, alternative media, social media, Twitter, Facebook, Google, and YouTube, they would overwhelmingly refuse to partake in the outright selling out of their country, their children and families, their property, their freedom, and their birthright.

Unfortunately, the fraud has come full circle. The American people are teetering at the brink of the abyss, and their nation and all it's worth are being sold on the chopping block for the benefit of the global deep state oligarchy/plutocracy, who all plan to bail on this great nation for hopes of a better future and tomorrow, without them, of course.

The American people will not abide by this, and they have duly elected Donald Trump because they truly believe that he will be the man who finally puts this outrageous, fraudulent, and fictitious debt down for good, either though outright cancellation, repudiation, or renegotiation, perhaps for pennies on the dollar.

And who will come to collect if the USA doesn't pay?

The United States of America is pound for pound the strongest, most militarily superior, most patriotic nation, where each and every one of its citizens is armed to the teeth, and we have tens of thousands of nuclear weapons.

As the Greek saying goes, *"Molon Labe"* (Come and take it). Usually this phrase refers to the refusal to relinquish weapons, but in this case, this could also refer to the US debt.

Donald Trump needs to reset the clock, reset the debt, link our currency to tangibles such as gold, real property, and silver instead of fiat fractional reserve paper promissory notes, and get on with "making America great again."

Deep State Members and Their Agents Are Slowly Revealing Themselves

On a daily basis, with increasing frequency, the various and individual members and agents of the Deep State are being forced to emerge from the shadows and reveal themselves in order to desperately save their new world order vision.

For the better part of the last seventy years, since the end of World War II, the proverbial US Deep State has gone through several changes/metamorphoses, starting with their initial inception as the literal Nazi intelligentsia, spies, medical doctors, scientists, eugenicists, social engineers, and other parasites of humanity when they were brought over to the United States in Operation Paperclip, in order to continue their surreptitious human rights violating programs under the full protection and aegis of a monied American elite, which desperately wanted to maximize their own personal power by adopting and arrogating unto themselves the poisonous fruit of the war criminals they brought over from the Third Reich.

Men like Sidney Gottlieb, Werner von Braun, Arthur Rudolph, and more than fifteen thousand others were immediately given new identities and papers and put to work in order to develop the Deep State, made up of some elements of the military-industrial complex, national security state, American police state, corrupt judiciary beholden to the international bankers and corporations rather than to the US Constitution or American People, and all the myriad social engineering programs designed to extricate and remove all elements of humanity from their subjugated masses, for ease of control, manipulation, and murder.

But the success of the American Deep State was predicated upon abject secrecy, and although they were infiltrated and interwoven with the Neoconservative elements starting in the late 1980s early 1990s, who were really just Trotskyite Communists imported from Soviet Russia, their goals were one and the same: a new world order, based on fear, intimidation, warmongering, draconian and tyrannical domestic and foreign policy, a deeply ingrained belief in their moral and intellectual superiority, and essentially Luciferian ideals that they were, in fact, gods on earth and could do what they pleased when and how they wanted.

This also meant taking upon themselves the power to kill and murder anyone at will, in the Luciferian motto of "Deus Meumque Jus," or "God according to my right," whether through indirect soft-kill methods such as social engineering, corruption, COINTELPRO, gang-stalking, or sanctions, or by outright direct murder, warfare, paramilitary operations, terrorism, assassination, and murder.

The last election saw President Donald Trump emerge as a product of the American people waking up with a steady stream of real-time news, social media updates from around the world, an interlocking of the world's people like has never occurred in modern history, and with the awakening of the entire world (and most significantly within the US and Europe), where the shadowy figures within the Deep State proponents of new world order globalism started to be thrust into the light, to reveal themselves as Gollum-like, hideous figures that lived, breathed, and died by death, destruction, bullying, and supreme arrogance.

However, as the American people started waking up from their slumber at having been sold out and manipulated steadily for the past seventy years, so too did the "useful" idiots and agents of the Deep State begin to wake up, and in so doing many of them began to throw off their shackles of agency and slavery of the bona fide members of the Deep State, often throwing their masters under the bus with countless and relentless intelligence leaks, blogs, alternative news media websites and forums, domestic and international communication, and otherwise bucking the tide and hurling their Deep State masters like an angry horse throwing off an abusive rider digging in his painful spurs.

In a panic, the Deep State is now beginning to realize that if you want to do it right, you have to do it yourself.

This means that the mainstream media, Twitter, Facebook, social media, and all other mechanisms of communication to the masses have now been heavily deluged by the actual treasonous Deep State actors themselves or their totally evil but committed agents who still demonstrate their loyalty (because they know that the truth is now firmly out there), these agents who are craving money, power, drugs, and sex (or are being blackmailed) rather than the welfare of their fellow citizenry or the tenets of the US Constitution and the guarantees of inalienable human and civil rights that it ensures.

So the low-level, ineffective emissaries of the Deep State are slowly being eliminated either because of their general incompetence or because they have refused to carry the water anymore, while others who are willing to reaffirm their deal with the devil are rapidly being promoted and exalted.

But if one pays attention, it is now becoming crystal clear, and especially during this time of massive intelligence investigations and hearings occurring on Capitol Hill, just who exactly these Deep State bastards really are.

They have a few messages and characteristics that distinguish them from ordinary, patriotic Americans:

(1) an overwhelming desire to start World War III by relentlessly attacking, provoking, demonizing, and vilifying otherwise isolated and relatively nonthreatening nations such as Russia, Iran, Syria, China, and other nations not towing the line;

(2) a deep commitment to financing and galvanizing the protected classes with their identity politics through their divide-and-conquer schemes to foment division, discord, and cacophony, rather than encouraging American solidarity, unity, brotherhood, patriotism, and cohesion;

(3) an alarming hatred of the alternative media, terming it fake news when it fails to echo the same canned bullshit as is vomited out of the mainstream news media outlets;

(4) incessant and relentless attacks on President Donald Trump, with the end game being his delegitimization, undermining, obstruction, impeachment, or much worse;

(5) an unflappable desire to reinforce and strengthen NATO while absorbing more nations into that Nazi sired behemoth (remember that Hitler's Army Chief Adolph Heusinger during the Nazi Third Reich eventually also became chairman of NATO, with the same goals and behaviors carried along with him);

(6) an unshakeable belief in and refusal to audit or abolish the Federal Reserve or to allow US Government coining of its own nation's currency;

(7) a deep commitment to the American Stasi-like police state with its attendant social engineering, manipulation of the judiciary and the courts, and complete and total control over the legislative (Congress and Senate), and if possible, domination and infiltration of the executive branch.

So the next time you watch the mainstream media or read a Tweet or social media blog, pay close attention to the statements and positions coming out of the purveyor's mouth or pen. You might just be looking straight into the eyes, or reading the words, of a bona fide member of the Deep State and enemy of the inalienable civil liberties and human rights of the American people, as guaranteed by the United States Constitution.

The United Nations Needs to Do Their Job

W ho is going to police the Deep State?

When a small band of Deep State criminals and hooligans can manage to literally hijack the most powerful country on earth, the United States of America, a land of three-hundred-million-plus people, replete with more than thirty to fifty thousand nuclear weapons, the most powerful military on earth, and with a GDP of 25 percent of the entire world's nations combined, and when this band of Deep State criminals literally control 99 percent of that nation's wealth to literally force its hand to do whatever they want all across the globe, even in the face of direct resistance and protests of 99.9 percent of that nation's governed people, it is time for someone or some entity to curb that international criminal behavior and conduct.

Right now, the United States three branches of government—the executive, legislative, and judiciary—have been completely co-opted and corrupted by the very few members of the money powered oligarch/plutocrat elite, to the point where day-to-day life for the governed US masses is laughable and the rest of the world's population is downright deadly and dangerous.

Even the current president of the United States, Donald Trump, who was elected and came to office riding the wave of populist American sentiment and revolt against this existential nightmare facing the American People, eventually found it useful and more expedient to completely abandon and ignore his three-hundred-million-plus American citizenry and instead opt to lob one hundred million dollars' worth of Tomahawk missiles into a sovereign nation, Syria, based wholly on incomplete and uninvestigated allegations from the same band of Deep State warmonger liars who embroiled the US and its allies into the 2003 Iraq war, based solely on falsified and politicized intelligence, bribery, lobbying, and mainstream media lockstep owned by the same Deep State oligarchs/plutocrats, resulting in tens of millions of people in Iraq and throughout the Middle East dead, displaced, with lives ruined for eternity.

It has now been firmly established with hard evidence that ISIS was formed, funded, and created by Western Intelligence (US CIA and British M-I6), plus other Gulf nations such as Saudi Arabia, Qatar, as well as Israel and

Turkey, to literally disrupt, disorient, destabilize, and destroy the secular governments throughout the Middle East so that they could install their own crony leadership to rule that area with the same corrupted, disturbing, and sick methodology as they rule their imprisoned people back in their home nations.

The United Nations has been in existence since 1948 and was founded upon the basic charter to protect human rights and inalienable civil liberties and the sovereign territorial integrity of all those 193 member nations, but to date has done absolutely nothing to either prevent or punish those international global war criminals and Mafia chieftains who openly thumb their nose and flout not only the UN but also the remaining 99 percent of the global population and their host nations/countries/leaders.

Article 1 of the UN Charter, entitled "Purposes of the United Nations," states that the adopted purposes of the United Nations is to essentially prohibit war (except in self-defense) by stating the following:

> All Members shall settle their international disputes by peaceful means in such a manner that international peace and security, and justice, are not endangered. All Members shall refrain in their international relations from the threat or use of force against the territorial integrity or political independence of any state, or in any other manner inconsistent with the Purposes of the United Nations.

The right to self-defense is reaffirmed in Article 51, which states the following:

> Nothing in the present Charter shall impair the inherent right of individual or collective self-defense if an armed attack occurs against a Member of the United Nations.

When international criminal conduct occurs, by extremely wealthy and powerful individuals, NGOs, and criminal oligarch/plutocratic entities, all throughout the world, affecting the territorial integrity or sovereign immunity of the world's people, the UN is presently and currently absolutely unwilling, or unable, to do a goddamned thing about it.

The UN apparently has no law enforcement or police power, and this could be the ultimate problem, because even if they wanted to punish a nation or individual who directly flouts international law, they can and will not do anything to enforce their hollow words and security resolutions.

The only portion of the UN Charter that remotely even touches on this issue pertains to Chapter VII of the United Nations Charter that sets out the UN Security Council's powers to maintain peace.

It allows the council to "determine the existence of any threat to the peace, breach of the peace, or act of aggression" and to take military and non-military action to "restore international peace and security."

Chapter VII also gives the Military Staff Committee responsibility for strategic coordination of forces placed at the disposal of the UN Security Council.

It is made up of the chiefs of staff of the five permanent members of the council.

The UN Charter's prohibition of member states of the UN attacking other UN member states is central to the purpose for which the UN was founded in the wake of the destruction of World War II—to prevent war.

This overriding concern is also reflected in the Nuremberg Trials' concept of a crime against peace, which is "starting or waging a war against the territorial integrity, political independence or sovereignty of a state, or in violation of international treaties or agreements" (crime against peace), which was held to be the crime that makes all war crimes possible.

Article 42 states the following:

> Should the Security Council consider that measures provided for in Article 41 would be inadequate or have proved to be inadequate, it may take such action by air, sea, or land forces as may be necessary to maintain or restore international peace and security. Such action may include demonstrations, blockade, and other operations by air, sea, or land forces of Members of the United Nations.

Article 51 provides for the right of countries to engage in self-defense, including collective self-defense, against an armed attack (including cyberattacks):

> Nothing in the present Charter shall impair the inherent right of individual or collective self-defense if an armed attack occurs against a Member of the United Nations, until the Security Council has taken measures necessary to maintain international peace and security. Measures taken by Members in the exercise of this right of self-defense shall be immediately reported to the

Security Council and shall not in any way affect the authority and responsibility of the Security Council under the present Charter to take at any time such action as it deems necessary in order to maintain or restore international peace and security.

Finally, Chapter XIV of the United Nations Charter deals with the International Court of Justice.

Most provisions related to the World Court are contained in the Statute of the International Court of Justice, which is annexed to the charter.

Article 93 states that all UN members are members of the World Court.

Article 94 requires all members to abide by World Court decisions in any cases to which they are a party and gives the UN Security Council power to enforce such decisions.

The World Court is also authorized to issue advisory opinions upon request.

Article 1, entitled "The Purposes of the United Nations," states the following:

> To maintain international peace and security, to take effective collective measures for the prevention and removal of threats to the peace, and for the suppression of acts of aggression or other breaches of the peace, and to bring about by peaceful means, and in conformity with the principles of justice and international law, adjustment or settlement of international disputes or situations which might lead to a breach of the peace;
>
> To develop friendly relations among nations based on respect for the principle of equal rights and self-determination of peoples, and to take other appropriate measures to strengthen universal peace;
>
> To achieve international co-operation in solving international problems of an economic, social, cultural, or humanitarian character, and in promoting and encouraging respect for human rights and for fundamental freedoms for all without distinction as to race, sex, language, or religion; and
>
> To be a center for harmonizing the actions of nations in the attainment of these common ends.

Article 2 states the following:

The Organization and its Members, in pursuit of the Purposes stated in Article 1, shall act in accordance with the following Principles:

The Organization is based on the principle of the sovereign equality of all its Members.

All Members, in order to ensure to all of them the rights and benefits resulting from membership, shall fulfill in good faith the obligations assumed by them in accordance with the present Charter.

All Members shall settle their international disputes by peaceful means in such a manner that international peace and security, and justice, are not endangered.

All Members shall refrain in their international relations from the threat or use of force against the territorial integrity or political independence of any state, or in any other manner inconsistent with the Purposes of the United Nations.

All Members shall give the United Nations every assistance in any action it takes in accordance with the present Charter, and shall refrain from giving assistance to any state against which the United Nations is taking preventive or enforcement action.

The Organization shall ensure that states which are not Members of the United Nations act in accordance with these Principles so far as may be necessary for the maintenance of international peace and security.

Nothing contained in the present Charter shall authorize the United Nations to intervene in matters which are essentially within the domestic jurisdiction of any state or shall require the Members to submit such matters to settlement under the present Charter; but this principle shall not prejudice the application of enforcement measures under Chapter VII of the United Nations Charter.

The United Nations, in their almost daily get-togethers, sitting around a table and voting on things, need to now use their 193-strong nation membership and take one final but essential vote—to give themselves the power and authority to investigate, arrest, detain, and incarcerate those international war criminals who directly flout their resolutions and rules and who bully other nations into submission by murdering, bombing, invading, disrupting, disorienting, raping, pillaging, terrorizing, and destroying other nations and their people simply because they have the money, power, and connections to do so.

This is the only way that global (and sovereign nation) peace can occur, when the UN finally grows a pair, steps up to the plate, and asserts itself as the final and ultimate arbiter of international justice and punishment of global criminal activity, emanating from only one or two hijacked rogue nation states in their repertoire and arsenal of member nations.

We Should Trust President Donald Trump

Donald Trump and his deep love for America has not changed since he became president of the United States. Only his knowledge and access to national security intelligence and information has.

With the recent Syrian tomahawk missile attack by the Trump administration after what appeared to have been dubious evidence of Syrian culpability, President Donald Trump lost a great deal of his loyal supporters and followers.

This is because tens of millions of Americans (as well as hundreds of millions of people overseas) felt that he was playing fast and furious in courting World War III, which is an unforgivable sin and hazard to play with the lives of eight billion human beings on planet earth.

Furthermore, his recent and seeming flip-flops on other issues, which contrasted so blatantly his passionate message blasts via Twitter for the past several years, also made Trump appear to be disingenuous, or even worse, dishonest, as well as an opportunist.

Many argued that Donald Trump was in fact always part of the Deep State, an insider who simply lied to the American people en masse in order to get elected.

However, is this really true?

We already know that Donald Trump is an America-firster who deeply and passionately cares about the United States and who wants to see his beloved nation do well. We know this because you simply cannot fake it that well for decades since he first began to do his interviews as a young man in his thirties, with some famous interviews with a young Tom Brokaw and even with Allen King, Oprah Winfrey, and Rona Barrett, among others.

What is striking in all these interviews is that in each and every one of them, Donald Trump comes across as a very kind, sweet, compassionate, intelligent, and concerned American citizen who cares deeply about his country and how well it does in the future.

He also makes it very clear in each and every one of these interviews that he would rather not be president of the United States, or run for office, because it is a very "mean life" and because he would rather see someone else more qualified to actually do the job correctly.

No one can fake that type of consistently sincere love for America and deep personal humility for more than four decades in public life starting when he was only thirty.

Donald Trump is the real deal and wants what is best for America, not for himself.

He truly wishes to spend his older years fixing and helping America become great again, like it was when he was a young man, and for this sentiment he should be lionized and commended, not criticized.

So what changed?

Why does it appear that he has flip-flopped on so many of his pre-election platforms and positions, most notably the much vaunted and posted retweets of his opposition to intervention in Syria or other issues?

Well, perhaps the best answer is now, President Donald Trump has number one top priority security clearance and has the information and intelligence at his fingertips, which has caused him to make certain decisions that he would not have made before, when he quite frankly did not know much more than the average American citizen, without the benefit of this raw intelligence and information.

The point is, Donald Trump and his deep love for America has not changed, merely his knowledge and awareness of what is ailing America has.

And this newfound knowledge of truths that are not shared with the American people on National Security grounds has altered and colored his decision-making and judgments.

So we as Americans must take comfort in the fact that we elected this great man to be our president because he resonated with us and convinced us of who he is and what he stands for.

And now, we must also trust President Donald Trump that he will continue to do what is best for the United States of America, and its people, even if we as Americans often do not quite understand why he has made some of these decisions in the first place.

USA Shooting Itself in
Foot with Sanctions Against Eurasia

The US Treasury Department and Legislature are not doing average Americans any favors by blacklisting, alienating, and sanctioning other oil/gas-rich, wealthy nations in Eurasia having burgeoning economies at the behest of their International Central Banker masters.

If average Americans could visit the sprawling countries of Eurasia, including Russia, Kazakhstan, Azerbaijan, Georgia, Armenia, Turkey, China, and other nations, they would quickly surmise that those nations are literally drenched in oil, gas, minerals, and natural resource wealth that are literally just begging to be developed and marketed in the international stream of commerce.

Brand-new buildings, with the latest advances in structural and physical ingenuity, dot the landscape of these nations, being commissioned and put up by the latest geniuses who brought us the towers in Dubai and other fabulously wealthy nations in the East, while the infrastructure and architecture of the United States and Great Britain lay in self-pleased antiquity and junky comparison.

The United States has always been a nation of progress, ingenuity, discovery, wonder, and periodic renewal in almost each and every capacity for growth and development, but for some reason, the kernel of genius and wisdom so carefully inserted into the US Constitution and Bill of Rights by the founding fathers has been subverted and stifled by the International Central Bankers and their minions within the executive, legislative, and judicial branch, as well as its lapdog corporate mainstream media, to literally prevent and paralyze America from joining in this absolute financial and economic boom currently underway in Eurasia.

Even though the United States has the most advanced technological abilities to fully assist and help develop the natural resources and markets of all the countries that the shortsighted and idiotic US Treasury Department on its own is waging a sanction war against, American corporations and its employees are being held back and kept out of the loop by various members of the US Government itself, who are often shareholders and members of the board of directors of those foreign companies from Eurasian nations who are, in fact, making a killing on these new and emerging and developing markets going on right now.

The stench and sickness of hypocrisy in denying the American citizenry the boons and benefits of this newfound wealth and natural resource prosperity by their US Treasury masters with idiotic and counterproductive sanctions is truly mind-boggling, while these governmental economic suppressors continue to take part in and financially benefit, through their own corporate and international cronyism, in these burgeoning industries.

These idiots within the US Treasury Department, using their half-educated nimrods within the US Congress and Senate, continue to pump out international economic stifling sanctions, seemingly 24 hours a day, 7 days a week, 365 days per year, under the idiotic appellation and specious banner of "combating international Islamic terrorism" against certain nations, which, if the USA actively encouraged trade and friendly relationships with, would yield untold and limitless bountiful economic fruit to all segments of the US economic sector and its people, but again, these harbingers of doom working within the US Government would rather deprive their fellow American citizenry while all the while having one foot in the Eurasian economic door through their international relationships overseas.

And international Islamic terrorism has also been revealed to be simply a disruptive boogeyman created, funded, armed, trained, and dispatched by our friendly neighborhood International Central bankers and their equally stoogelike Intelligence Services for precisely this purpose, to foment conflict, division, and provocation so that they can use variously selected, idiotic, and shortsighted world leaders to sanction, embargo, invade, and terrorize other world nations not towing the proverbial line of their international and global agenda.

For example, in Azerbaijan, Georgia, Kazakhstan, and other oil/gas-rich nations, we are constantly repressing and sanctioning integral nations such as Iran, Russia, Syria, Belarus, Balkans, China, Kyrgyzstan, Venezuela, and scores of other nations who are being idiotically alienated and provoked with financially crippling US embargoes and sanctions instead of enjoying full diplomatic relations in the spirit of working together, thus hitting all Americans directly where it counts the most—in their pocket book.

George Washington, in his farewell address, stated that "it is our true policy to steer clear of permanent alliance with any portion of the foreign world."

Thomas Jefferson, at his inauguration, pledged "peace, commerce, and honest friendship with all nations-entangling alliances with none."

It is quite striking when one of our most powerful and wealthy American companies, Boeing, cannot even sell its passenger airplanes to a country like Iran, potentially making trillions of dollars and creating hundreds of thousands of high-paying US jobs just because a handful of disloyal and crony members of the US Treasury and their minions in the US Legislature carry out their bidding and prevent them all from doing business, thus driving this massively lucrative business and jobs creation directly into the hands of Airbus, Europe's number one passenger airline company, to the tune of trillions of dollars in current and future revenue.

But this is only one example out of thousands of US corporations and foreign nations that they target.

But our counterproductive sanctions and embargoes against so many different nations, under the dubious guise of terrorism, rather than through direct problem-solving, conflict resolution, and resolute negotiation procedures through diplomacy and communication, are having the ultimate and pernicious effect of leaving America in the economic and financial dirt, while augmenting and increasing the economic and logistical development of the nations (and their friends) that we are targeting.

However, this might be the grand game and goal of the International Central bankers in their international economic chess game in the first place.

Great World Powers Should Not Remain Oblivious of Internal Corruption of Other Nations Global World Leaders Should Never Turn a Blind Eye to the Internal Crimes and Corruption of Other World Leaders

In a vain attempt to streamline global new world order governance, it is sometimes very tempting for macro world leaders to simply implement domestic and global policies that completely steam roll over the rights of their individual citizens for purposes of ease of control and rule rather than taking the time out to deal with, and rectify, the multiple internecine conflicts, fundamental denials of human and civil rights, race/religious/ethnic tensions, and rampant injustices which plague their people.

This type of behavior is the mark of a lazy world leader, and their best defense from outside scrutiny and criticism of the methods they use to quash their own people's hopes and dreams is by knee-jerk declaring that they are protected from outside scrutiny by the doctrine of sovereign immunity, which is an international law concept declaring that a country has the absolute right to monitor and control their own internal domestic policies and procedures without outside influence and interference from other sovereign nations.

However, what happens when that small handful of influential, powerful, and wealthy global world leaders are business partners, friends, cronies, or connected to those other equally culpable world leaders?

How is that 5 or 6 global world leaders, with any degree of power and wealth, can stifle and crush the hopes and dreams of the 8 billion people in the world?

The disappointments, human and civil liberties tramplings, and deeply ingrained and systemic corruption, endemic within much of the world's countries, is not something to simply brush aside and cover up, under the guise of smooth global governance and streamlining, and must be closely monitored by other nations.

In this vein, once again, the United Nations must do its job.

At least within the United Nations, there are 193 member nations that all have leaders who can actually do something about these issues.

The US/West/Russia Need to
Stop Picking Sides in the Middle East

S top picking sides in the Middle East, arming one against another.

Picking sides and arming/funding/training competing sides of Middle Eastern Islamic terrorist groups and nations by the US/West/Russia has to come to an end, and a common strategy and close working relationship need to be established.

This ludicrous game of international whack a-mole that the US/West/ Russian intelligence and military services seem to be playing with international terrorism has to come to a resounding end, with the disgusting and revolting attacks on little girls attending an Ariana Grande concert in Manchester England yesterday.

If this is not the final alarm bell designed to wake up the respective governments of the United States, Western European nations, and the Russian Federation to stop picking sides in the Middle East, arming one against another, swimming through the murky waters of ISIS, moderate rebels, alQaeda, al-Nusra, Hamas, Hezbollah, and other fundamentalist Islamic paramilitary organizations, then nothing else could be.

It is high time that the US/West/Russia demand that the Sunni-dominated Gulf State nations (Saudi Arabia, Qatar, UAE, Turkey), as well as the Shiadominated Eurasian Islamic nations such as Syria and Iran, acquiesce to and accept intelligence and military officers within their own respective governments to monitor, be aware and appraised of, and informed of all comings and goings within their countries involving terrorism, militancy, and other scourges of humanity designed to disrupt and disorient innocent communities within the US/West/Russia.

This is not to advocate a full-scale war against any of these Islamic nations, as the Neocons/Neoliberals would suggest, but rather a peaceful offer and one they cannot (and should not) refuse.

Peacefully admit and allow representatives from the ranks of the intelligence and military communities of these three entities (US/West/Russia) to work closely with the indigenous governments of the Shia and Sunni dominated sects of Islam to clamp down, monitor, and prevent global international terrorism, wherever it should manifest itself.

This way, if another terrorist attack should unfortunately occur on the soil of the US/West/Russia again, then those governments were either complicit in it or were asleep at the wheel.

Either way, blame and accountability can and should be assigned, and punishments by the people against their leadership should ensue.

The time for political correctness is over, the time for the defense of sovereign immunity of nation states is over, and it is time to get serious in the fight on the scourge of international terrorism.

The message from the US/West/Russian Federation to the Shia/Sunni world should be this:

Either voluntarily admit a sufficient number of intelligence/military officers/personnel into your respective governments to inspect (just like the IAEA and UN are allowed to periodically inspect their nuclear/weapons facilities) and monitor in order to prevent the burgeoning training, funding, organization, coordination, arming, and planning of international terrorism, or be destroyed in outright warfare.

Because the USA/West/Russia should no longer accept the horrific and disturbing deaths of their own civilians on their own home territory (especially little girls going to a concert in the middle of England).

The people Must Be Leery of Strengthening Terrorists within Own Governments in Fight against Terrorism

While it is tempting to get carried away in the outrage and emotionalism brought on by the recent terrorist attacks in the United Kingdom, France, and other parts of Europe, the people must also be cautious about inadvertently strengthening the countless bad apples within their respective governments in their intelligence agencies, law enforcement, and governments by giving them even more legal power to terrorize their own citizens with impunity.

Although the vast majority of federal and state law enforcement can safely be declared to be decent, hardworking, honorable men and women keeping law and order within their respective nations, the fact remains that there are also an awful lot of bad, indecent, cruel, power-hungry, greedy, violent, dishonest, and criminal elements also within their ranks.

In fact, the vast majority of criminal and terrorist acts committed against the citizenry is without a doubt emanating from those bad apple within federal and state law enforcement, armed fully with the color and power of the law, hiding and obfuscating their evil acts under the banner of the badge.

The ratio of criminal and terrorist acts committed against the population by federal and state law enforcement to radical Islamic or other types of politically based terrorists is approximately 1,000,000 to 1.

So to ignore that basic statistic is extremely dangerous, given the fact that the mainstream media and even the world's population (including undersigned author) are up in arms lately about the back to back recent terrorist acts having occurred in the United Kingdom, France, and the rest of Europe, demanding that their countries' law enforcement, intelligence services, and governments begin to immediately stamp out all vestiges of international and domestic Islamic and other types of politically based organized terrorism.

However, the United States has seen an unprecedented level of illegal surveillance, fabricated terror attacks by federal and state law enforcement, eradication of the bill of rights and human civil liberties, a literal police state having been formed since the mid-1940s, but picking up steam and solidifying openly after the attacks of September 11, 2001, and at this point, things could not get much worse with regards to the overall undermining of the United States Constitution, not by international Islamic terrorists, but by the prostitutes in government within the legislative, executive, and judiciary branches of the US government.

So while it is tempting to demand safety for increased security, one must also be eternally cognizant and vigilant that we also vet, closely scrutinize, and supervise those members of the intelligence community, federal, and state law enforcement, and various members of the military industrial complex and national security state, in order to ensure that although we are now about to give them even greater powers and latitude to protect us from terrorism, that we do not also accidentally allow those bad apples within those respective agencies to enable them to even better gang-stalk, harass, do surveillance, provoke, set up, frame, and target us as citizens, even worse than they are doing now.

The Importance of Maintaining Humanity in the Struggle to Remain Free

It is only when the world's people collectively forget their own individual humanity will their eternal global enslavement be accomplished by the global oligarchs.

It is now a sign of success and well adjustment to be completely and totally sociopathic in the modern day developed first world.

If one exhibits any semblance of humanity or compassion, one is considered altogether weak and not fully adapted to the consumer-driven culture of the current age, where not only are articles of manufacture, agricultural products, natural resources, and other inanimate objects having intrinsic value measured by their capitalistic worth, but also the very people themselves, who inhabit the earth.

In this modern day, every man, woman, and child has now been ascribed an inherent value, in monetary terms, and their humanity is at once mitigated, if not completely removed, when factoring their worth in the world.

This is indeed the first beginning phase of a near-certain brave new world in which the global oligarchs/plutocrats are preparing the majority of humanity for near chattel-like status, only ending in abject and pure slavery, wherein their entire existence is only to please their global masters and service their needs.

This reality has not yet hit the majority of the earth's people, because if it did, there would already be mass pandemonium, revolution, and overthrow of the oligarchs/plutocrats and their prostitutes in all of the world's governments who are responsible for slowly boiling the proverbial frog through the subtle, yet deadly, implementation of their policies and laws.

The key to saving humanity from eternal slavery is the immediate recognition of the inherent worth and humanity of each of the people on earth and a wholehearted resistance to accepting and growing accustomed to the worthlessness and marginalization being foisted upon them by the global oligarchs/plutocrats.

This is indeed the greatest battle of all—the struggle for earth's people to remember and keep at the forefront of their minds their individual greatness and divinity (humanity) within.

At the end of the day, no amount of techno-tyranny being slowly erected around the masses by the global oligarchs can crush the human spirit, provided, of course, that the people fight to keep it.

This is another reason why the oligarchs favor drugging the masses through massive and organized legal (and illegal) opioid dispensation, because it is a lot easier to control the masses when they have been dehumanized in the first place.

This is also the reason why the oligarchs have abolished the homeschooling mechanism, opting instead to forcibly mandate all the world's children to attend government sponsored and designed educational programs, which, by design, are meant to quell, crush, stunt, and dumb down even the most curious and intellectually powerful of the world's youth.

The Hindu philosophy advocates two forms of divinity within the world: that of the Brahma, i.e., divinity external to the human experience, and that of the Atma, representing the inherent divinity existing individually within us all.

It is the latter, the Atma, which is what the world's people must cling to, and guard jealously, if they are to maintain their individual freedoms and ability to choose their own destinies by first recognizing and then overthrowing and banishing the tyrants within their midst.

Recognition of evil in global society in the form of human oligarch enslavers absolutely requires a keen ability to become introspective and tap into one's humanity in order to gauge the external enemy attempting to enslave.

Unfortunately, since the world is on a fast trajectory toward total consumerism of the human entity, at great cost and effectiveness by the world's enslavers, it will always be a struggle to hold on to that humanity, but in the end, this chalice of the human spirit can, and must, endure in order for the world's people to remain free (and alive) into eternity.

The End of Muslim Sunni-Shia Hospitality
The Qatar-Iran Alliance Brokered by France

Economics and human practicality have finally triumphed over backward superstition and religious dogma underlying the Sunni-Shia conflict, which has caused hundreds of millions of unnecessary deaths, war, global terrorism, and destruction over the past few hundred years.

In a hugely symbolic victory of sound economics and practicality triumphing over stupid, backward, and idiotic sectarian violence and religious and ethnic discrimination, the French oil-refining company Total has successfully brokered a joint oil drilling / natural gas development deal with Qatar (Sunni-dominated) and Iran (Shia-dominated) as joint partners.

Only a few weeks ago, Saudi Arabia (source of Sunni aggression in the Middle East) and the rest of the Gulf Cooperation Council (GCC) issued a stern warning to Qatar not to get into bed with or do business with Iran, a Shia-dominated country who has been mercilessly attacked, vilified, and isolated from the rest of the Middle East, Europe, and United States at the behest of Saudi Arabia and its ally Israel.

The list of demands handed by Saudi Arabia and the GCC (backed by the US and Israel) to Qatar, given only one week to comply, was altogether unrealistic, ridiculous, overarching, overbearing, and all at once impossible to comply with (e.g., closing down the *Al Jazeer*a news network, which is the only relatively free media operation in the Gulf State area).

Now the Russian news outlet *Duran* reports in their new article "Qatar, Iran, a French Gas Company and One Natural Gas Field" that Qatar and Iran have together openly flouted Saudi Arabia (and the rest of the GCC, US, and Europe) to work together in the spirit of economics, practicality, independence, individuality, and mutual cooperation to develop energy together with a leading European nation, France, for the benefit of their respective nations.

Few people understand the massive and earth-shattering global ramifications of such a development. This is literally the beginning of the end of the openly hostile, violent, destructive, and disruptive Shia-Sunni Islamic conflict, which has ravaged the Muslim world for the past few hundred years, resulting in untold death, destruction, war, terrorism, and disturbance to the Middle East and the rest of the world, killing hundreds of millions of people.

This Sunni-Shia conflict has also been successfully exploited and used by countless countries, intelligence agencies, unscrupulous businessmen, and individuals all across the planet to line their own pockets with gold and silver, all at the expense of the world and its security.

Those nations representing the P5+1 (United Kingdom, China, Russia, Germany, USA, France) that helped to negotiate, broker, crystallize, and then finalize the Iran Nuclear Agreement can now sit back and smile triumphantly as that deal literally paved the way for such a monumental development and achievement for humanity, peace in the Middle East, and diplomacy, rather than outright war, cacophony, destruction, war, terrorism, and death all across the world.

Human reasoning and insight has overcome the idiotic superstitions and hocus-pocus discrimination held by generations of people in the Middle East to try and preserve the world and avoid World War III.

Now let's see who tries to dissuade and derail this burgeoning French-Iran-Qatar oil/gas development deal, as they will then have revealed themselves to in fact be the enemies of humanity and the source of global wars and destruction to begin with for the past few hundred years, responsible for the deaths of untold countless innocent souls.

America Is Not Simply Western Civilization But All Civilizations America Was Not Made Great by Western Civilization but Rather by all Civilization

M uch like Adam Garrie declared in his recent seminal article in the news periodical the *Duran*, entitled "5 Reasons American Foreign Policy Is Insanely Dangerous and Dangerously Insane," undersigned author is also a loyal Trump supporter, mainly for the reasons echoed in that piece in that Donald Trump appears to be a refreshing break from the past, a proverbial bull in a china shop, where the Deep State of global oligarchy/plutocracy would get the much deserved comeuppance that they deserve for decades, if not centuries, of misguided foreign policy, mass murdering of innocents both foreign and domestic, and exploitation and extortion of smaller countries and less-advantaged races/religions /ethnicities.

For many of us who supported Donald Trump, it was for the return of America to the fundamental notions of its founding fathers with a clear, delineated Bill of Rights and a US Constitution that guaranteed freedom, equality, respect, and liberty to all regardless of race, color, religion, or creed.

So it was with a slight grimace of pain to watch President Donald Trump stand side by side with the Polish president, in front of millions of Polish people, crowing on about Western civilization, preserving Western values, and guaranteeing that Western people would thrive and endure, never be broken, and that Western civilization would triumph.

The fact remains that the United States of America is, and has always been, run and sustained by a vast majority of people who did not hail from the West, nor have Western values, whatever that is.

The secret of America's greatness has always been the filling of jobs and roles and responsibilities in its admittedly Western infrastructure, such as its courts, police force, legislature, transportation system, industry, and other arenas by people from all over the world who have loaned their hard work, industriousness, diligence, thirst to succeed, and ingenuity to advancing America's interests both domestically, as well as all over the world.

And the truth of the matter is America's infrastructure and legal incorporation documents, while admittedly drafted by Western men

46

predominantly of Anglo-Saxon heritage, those documents were either based on, or completely borrowed/stolen from, other non-Western civilizations and great cultures that predated England and Germany by centuries, if not thousands of years.

The speech by Donald Trump tried conveniently to take credit for America's greatness by labeling it Western civilization, when in fact it completely discounted the massive and great contributions (past, present, and future) of, for example, the Jews (Middle Eastern and Eurasian people); the Chinese who built the railroads and transportation system; the Africans who built the entire infrastructure of the nation since before its founding with their blood sweat and tears before, during, and after slavery; the spirit of American independence and respect/love for nature given to us by the Native Americans; the ingenuities to science/technology/software production by the Indians, Chinese, and other Asians who left their birth nations in their great brain drains to bestow their genius upon the American economy and leadership in global technology and science; the Latin Americans who often feed and grow America's food supply amongst other major contributions; and the countless other ethnic/religious/racial groups not hailing from the proverbial West having Western values that make up the American fabric and cannot, and should not, be discounted or dismissed, as they are in fact the secret to America's greatness, not just the people who make up the society of Poland.

This is why Poland and the rest of Europe languishes in second world status, while the United States of America literally created, and defined, first world status.

America cannot solely be considered part and parcel of Western civilization, as that is completely and totally disrespectful and diminishes the achievements, genius, hard work, devotion, loyalty, and bona fide existence of the 90 percent of America who did not come from or hail from the Western world.

If America does not come to terms with this fact, it will soon be eclipsed and left behind when all the rest of the world finally figures out that they don't need Western civilization to move forward and progress anyway and, in fact, would probably do better without it.

Donald Trump Jr. Did Nothing Wrong by Collecting Criminal Information on Hillary Clinton from Any Source

D onald Trump Jr. did nothing wrong by collecting potential criminally incriminating information about a prospective presidential candidate Hillary Clinton from any source, as this would protect the American people, the United States of America, and further the interests of law enforcement and justice.

It is a well-known corollary of criminal law that an informant, or anyone who has information about a crime, has near blanket immunity to collect/report/release that information, even if it is against a powerful presidential candidate.

Additionally, anyone possessing information of a criminal nature can, and should, report it / bring it to the attention of law enforcement authorities, even if that party is a lawyer working with, or for, a foreign government, even if that were true, which at this point it really is not.

This was by no means election interference by a foreign government at all, because anybody could theoretically produce such incriminating information.

Even low-level criminal informants, drug dealers, prostitutes, private investigators, and witnesses can and should report errant criminal behavior to authorities, and this cannot be considered election interference in any sense of the word, as it is simply gaining and providing information in order to protect the American people from electing a criminal to office.

It is no secret that the Russian government preferred Donald Trump over Hillary Clinton to be president, because Hillary had already publicly vowed to destroy Russia and her allies and had already done so in Ukraine.

Providing evidence of a criminal nature, even if true, to her opposition candidate is only self-preservation, while assisting the American people in knowing just who exactly their prospective president is, and is certainly not election interference or a crime, or even unethical.

The latest look of outright glee and twinkles in the eyes of such loathsome Democrat politicians as Chuck Schumer and Adam Schiff on this latest news development betrays and belies their obvious conflict of interest in that they would rather see a criminal case / investigation obstructed, and evidence of criminal wrongdoing hidden, in order to protect their favored candidate, Hillary Clinton, rather than see justice done and the target of this criminal evidence revealed to the American people and law enforcement, and this is classic obstruction of justice, witness tampering, intimidation of a witness, and criminal interference with a bona fide criminal investigation.

The Democrats are up to their eyeballs in doing the exact same thing to Donald Trump, with information gleaned and gained from foreign intelligence services such as allegedly Israel and certain of its oligarchs/plutocrats, in order to have torpedoed the budding presidential candidacy of Donald Trump, and so their feigned outrage is more akin to Captain Renault in Casablanca who was "shocked, shocked, that gambling was going on here."

It is high time for the American people to demand that the real obstructionists and criminals in government office be thrown out or jailed immediately, i.e., the idiots who are reveling in concealing criminal activity by the Hillary Clinton camp, rather than by Donald Trump and his kids.

President Donald Trump Is Contending with and Defeating the Deep State Mainstream Media

President Donald Trump has single-handedly restored the First Amendment to the US Constitution by slamming and challenging the long-stagnant, established Deep State mainstream media, while supporting and championing the alternative media in the United States of America.

President Donald Trump has now successfully won over much of the major mainstream media, and the ones that he hasn't are struggling against the ropes, defending their entire existence as mouthpieces for the Deep State with their fake news.

The sheer tenacity, power, and positive attitude of President Trump, as a seasoned New York City businessman, are indeed serving him well.

He has also helped to launch and facilitate the alternative media, which is also now rapidly becoming the new mainstream media, with these outlets now enjoying thousands of times more viewers and consumers than their decades-long stagnant mainstream media competition.

In this vein, the First Amendment to the US Constitution is in full swing, where the honest and open alternative media, once stifled and sabotaged by the mainstream media in decades past, has now been given legs and support from the White House like at no other time in US history.

And his enemies in the mainstream media are literally running for cover at the America-first titan that they have unwittingly unleashed.

This is the essence of a free press, where one or two dedicated journalists, not being blessed with any bank loans or cash from wealthy cronies, but just simply having passion for the media and free speech, can literally launch an alternative non–mainstream media outlet and actually enjoy a full, rewarding, and strong career, rather than one eked out in the shadows, under the heavy thumb and antagonism of the established mainstream media outlets.

Additionally, various alternatives to the major search engines and social media sites, having already been proven to have been openly supported, funded, and allied with the Deep State, are also beginning to emerge, manned and gunned by some of the brightest and most innovative minds and imaginations of our nation's best and brightest.

Anyone who falsely pontificates that President Donald Trump is at war with the media is sorely misinformed. If anything, President Donald Trump may have saved the First Amendment and media in the United States as we know it by injecting new life, competition, alternative viewpoints, love, and respect for the US Constitution and the rule of law, as well as a deep and abiding love for the United States of America.

Mexican Oligarchs and Other Nations Need to Fix Own Economy and Stop Dumping People on USA

Americans must demand that the super wealthy oligarchs of foreign nations like Mexico dumping their people illegally into the USA must be held accountable for the destruction that they wreak, not just the poor people who have no choice but to flee.

The very sad news emanating out of San Antonio, Texas, today relates to a semi-tractor trailer filled to the brim with scores of illegal aliens from Mexico who literally died from heat exposure where their heart rates were reported to be over 130 beats per minute and their bodies were "hot to the touch," as reported by Texas law enforcement.

How is this possible?

Why do we read stories countless times per year about countries such as China, Vietnam, Mexico, or other nations having people who would literally risk death and dismemberment to illegally cross over their borders/shores to enter the United States and Europe?

While countries like Libya, Syria, and Yemen have an immediate excuse in that their countries were recently bombed to demolition by the evil forces behind NATO and other greedy Western Intelligence agencies who wanted to stunt those countries' growth, movement toward sovereign non–IMF / World Bank currencies, or to topple their duly elected sovereign leaders, what excuse does Mexico and other nations not having been immediately attacked or demoted by the Western nations have?

The answer is no excuse, whatsoever.

Mexico, for example, is literally loaded to the brim with cash, much of it ill-gotten gains from their massive illegal opioid, cocaine, marijuana, ecstasy, crystal meth, and painkiller trade, but also the vast majority of their economy is in the legal trade such as through coffee, avocados, produce, building materials, minerals, aerospace, electronics, food, beverages, tobacco, chemicals, iron, steel, petroleum, mining, textiles, clothing, motor vehicles, consumer durables, and tourism.

The economy of Mexico is the 13th largest in the world in nominal terms and the 11th largest by purchasing power parity, according to the International Monetary Fund.

Their GDP is $1.5 trillion (nominal 2016) and $2.5 trillion (PPP 2016).

Their GDP has been growing at 3 percent per year and is stable.

In 2016, Mexico exported $359.3 billion in drugs, automobiles, electronics, televisions, computers, mobile phones, LCDs, oil and oil products, silver, fruits, vegetables, coffee, and cotton all over the world.

So where is all this money going?

Why are their people routinely being forced to jump the border and literally risk their lives, and the lives of their small children, to illegally enter the United States and other nations?

The answer can be found in the Mexican oligarchy/plutocracy, which is obviously greedy and selfish beyond reproach.

Mexico should be a lesson to the United States and other nations that allow their internal oligarchs/plutocrats to grow without any pruning or trimming by their general population, or their corrupted governmental agencies such as the Federal Trade Commission (FTC).

While the Mexican upper class literally swims in money, their poorest classes must die like animals within trailer trucks in places like San Antonio, Texas, or languish in prisons both in Mexico (or in the United States) trying to desperately escape their horrific poverty and hellish living conditions.

The USA must not only punish and jail those illegal aliens who brave the elements to escape into the USA by jailing them or turning them back to Mexico but also come down like a hammer on the heads of those greedy bastard oligarchs in Mexico who do not give a damn about their own people and young children, rather allowing (and encouraging) them to sneak into the USA and other countries to risk their freedom and very lives.

"Make America Great Again"
Should Not Mean Rolling Back Human Rights
Awareness and Progress

P resident Donald Trump should be careful that his careless words do not roll back the enormous strides in human rights and civil liberties awareness and progress put into place by the previous President Barack

Obama administration over eight years, which sought to redress the deeply entrenched human rights violations and law enforcement misconduct within the American psyche of the past five hundred years, both domestically and overseas.

For all the faults of the previous President Barack Obama administration, mainly created by various elements of which he had little to no control over, one cannot deny that President Barack Obama made enormous strides in addressing and redressing the historic and deeply entrenched human rights violations existing within the American psyche and system since its inception and founding hundreds of years ago.

Conflating and confusing the recently augmented anger and angst that the American people had with regards to their failing and struggling economy, the resentment at globalism and waiting on line on the world stage with regards to many issues, and the rapid evaporation of American youth's desire to at least live as well as their parents or grandparents did should never occur with regard to the great progress America made over the past eight years relating to at least an awareness to combating rampant police and law enforcement abuse and misconduct, egregious human rights violations, the overarching surveillance state, tense race relations, epidemic corruption and unfairness within the courts, and other serious human rights concerns in America.

Recent news events indicate that the Trump administration is making moves that appear to be severely draconian and jackbooted with regards to law and order, and this should concern all Americans.

For example, in the news articles "Trump Tells Police Not to Worry about Injuring Suspects During Arrests" and "Trump Names Homeland Security Secretary John Kelly as White House Chief of Staff Ousting Reince Priebus," it truly looks like the country is moving rapidly away from human rights and progress and quickly devolving into an outright tyranny, police state, and fascism.

While these comments may be hyperbole, this type of loose banter by a sitting president cannot be allowed by the American people to continue unabated and is extremely dangerous as it most definitely will inspire federal and state law enforcement to increase and augment their already sick and troubling record of egregious human rights violations both here and abroad.

Only this past week the FBI arrested a Suffolk County Long Island Police officer Kevin McCoy who forced a young woman who only had a few outstanding traffic ticket warrants into giving him oral sex within his police precinct itself, completely and totally confident that he would be protected by the words and culture being created by Donald Trump and others in his administration.

Even President Obama's well-intended but poorly implemented universal health care originated from a good place, one where he and tens of millions of other Americans were frankly embarrassed that one of the richest and greatest countries in the world, the United States, could not (or would not) promise their people health care while the rest of the civilized world had long ago evolved beyond this.

The enormous strides made domestically with regards to at least the awareness that America has a deep-seated and deeply embedded human rights / race problem was finally thrust into the light when under President Barack

Obama, the heads of the US Department of Justice, Attorney Generals' office, Department of Homeland Security, and National Security Agency were all at some point led by minorities in America, predominantly African American, in order to at least make an attempt at equalizing the playing field and righting the wrongs of the past five hundred years of American mainland history right from the top on down.

But there was not enough time to fix it all.

Eight years was simply not enough.

President Donald Trump rose to office because there was a great deal of backlash, anger, and indeed hatred from a great many Americans who felt that they were left out of the globalist loop and disinvited from the proverbial elitist dinner table during those eight years, and they felt rightfully angered about it.

But all Americans must also remember that the human rights work, progress, awareness, and legislation of the previous Obama administration also ultimately ameliorated and bettered their situations as well.

Because when even one class of Americans is disenfranchised, alienated, and ostracized, then all Americans will eventually also become victims by the powers that be.

Only US Deep State Oligarchs
Want World War III

As long as Deep State oligarchs continue to use the Citizens United Supreme Court case to bribe entire US Congress and Senate 100 percent and shut out American citizen voters with hundreds of billions of dollars to one, President Donald Trump will never be able to accomplish anything for the American people.

It's truly time to pin the blame on the parties/individuals responsible for, on a near daily basis, bringing the world to the brink of nuclear war in World War III.

Because of the serious nature of their constant provocations, it is no longer acceptable for these mysterious, cowardly, and elusive figures to find peace and solace in the shadows of anonymity. For the sake of humanity, these bastards pushing the world to the brink of death and destruction in World War III need to be outed, and identified, now.

They allow the US Congress and Senate to take the blame for such horrific travesties as passing new provocative sanctions against Russia, Iran, North Korea, and other nations, which are completely and totally designed to provoke conflict.

They were also behind the provocations in the Ukraine, Syria, Libya, Yemen, Iraq, Africa, Eurasia, and Europe, resulting in billions of people dead or displaced.

Already the European Union has openly rebelled against these latest American unilateral sanctions because the USA is supposed to first consult with and obtain permission before engaging in global activity that could destroy the European economy.

These new sanctions threaten the liquefied natural gas industries being cultivated and grown by the Russia/Germany Nord Star 2 pipeline, as well as Turkish excursions relating to oil/gas into Europe.

However, the US government has decided to cripple not only its enemies but also its friends.

America-firsters need to also recognize and understand that a certain degree of globalism and international cooperation is absolutely essential for their own national security. Otherwise, America is just behaving like a spoiled kid in the playground, whose inevitable fate is a bloodied noise by the other kids.

The only problem here is that the proverbial bloody nose would in fact be thermonuclear war ending in World War III and the end of humanity.

Many sage and astute observers and analysts have now traced the latest bout of sanctions passed this week and signed by President Donald Trump today entirely to the massive lobbying and monetary power of the energy sector and military-industrial complex.

The question is, did they collude?

How much money was given to the loathsome members of the US Congress and Senate to bribe their vote for near-certain human extinction?

While the US Congress and Senate members take most, if not all, of the blame for pushing the world around, knocking out sovereign governments resulting in tens of millions of innocents dead, cacophony and chaos all over the world, massive human displacement and refugee crises numbering in the hundreds of millions, disappeared children in the hundreds of thousands, and other evil results, the oligarch puppet masters behind the scenes in the United States and around the world continue to go about their business, spending time with their families, living in their luxury homes, driving their elite automobiles, sending their kids to the top private schools and Ivy League universities, swimming in limitless amounts of liquid capital, above the law, and generally enjoying complete and total immunity from the people, families, children, cities, civilizations, and countries around the world whom they kill and destroy with sociopathic abandon.

Politicians as a rule are nothing but prostitutes, more so in the United States than in any other country, because lobbying is an accepted practice and has been justified as being constitutional in such landmark US Supreme Court decisions as *Citizens United v. FEC*, which allowed international corporations and international banks to successfully overpower financially all regular American citizens combined to achieve their lobbying goals and to pursue their own interests rather than the citizenry's interests.

There quite simply is no match, and the American people were rendered powerless and leaderless after this court decision, and their three hundred million collective voices were completely and totally blotted out in one swoop.

A dissenting opinion by Justice Stevens was joined by Justice Ginsburg, Justice Breyer, and Justice Sotomayor stating that the court's ruling "threatens to undermine the integrity of elected institutions across the Nation … The path it has taken to reach its outcome will … do damage to this institution." Justice Stevens concluded his dissent with the following:

> At bottom, the Court's opinion is thus a rejection of the common sense of the American people, who have recognized a need to prevent corporations from undermining self-government since the founding, and who have fought against the distinctive corrupting potential of corporate electioneering since the days of Theodore Roosevelt. It is a strange time to repudiate that common sense. While American democracy is imperfect, few outside the majority of this Court would have thought its flaws included a dearth of corporate money in politics.

So quite simply, the fact that the American people overwhelmingly came out to support and vote for Donald Trump to be president really made no difference anyway, since these mega corporations / international banks simply only need to buy the hell out of each and every whorish member of the US Congress and Senate and include a provision in the bill disallowing the people's elected president to veto their bill, and they can then literally shove any and all of their anti-American and pro–World War III bills and legislation down the American people's collective throats, exposing them all to death, destruction, and nuclear obliteration.

This all the while these bastard oligarchs have hundreds of multibillion-dollar homes / underground bunkers scattered throughout the world that they can jet off to at the first sign of nuclear war.

Scientists say that only cockroaches would survive a thermonuclear holocaust—well, maybe the oligarchs within the energy sector, military-industrial complex, and international banking industries, using the *Citizens United* case decision to completely and totally bypass the American people's will (and the will of the people of the European Union, Russia, Eurasia, Middle East, and Africa), share more in common with the cockroach than most people recognize.

These Deep State oligarchs will simply rinse, lather, and repeat each and every time President Donald Trump ever tries to do anything that he promised for the American people that the oligarchs either don't like or that they wish to use as a bargaining chip in order for him to get their support on something else.

This is a clarion call to the world's people to identify and out these craven oligarch sociopaths once and for all, for being the enemies of humanity that they are.

NYC Deep State Government Plays Politics while Subway Riders Suffer

L ike Nero during the fall of the Roman Empire, NYC's political Deep State plays the proverbial fiddle, bickering and infighting, while the people, dependent on the subway system, burn in squalor.

In one of their latest hidden games of nefarious politics, the New York City Deep State local government continues to bicker, sabotage, and undercut one another, using the most visible and sensitive aspects of Big Apple life, the MTA Subway System.

One only has to have ridden the subway in the last few months to notice that something has gone seriously wrong with everyday usage.

It is not uncommon, and in fact, it is now normal, to witness the following issues while taking your local subway by and between any of the five major boroughs within New York City:

(1) monstrous delays multiplying commuter time by five to ten times their normal stretch, stalling the NYC economy and making people miss work, appointments, or meetings;

(2) air-conditioning on the subway cars being nonexistent on the hottest summer days, with heating being equally absent during the coldest winter months;

(3) various lights fused, nonreplaced, on nearly all the subway cars, leaving passengers depressed and psychologically freaked out, having to stare at dark foreboding shadows all over the place;

(4) dirt, garbage, and filth plaguing the subway cars, as well as on the surrounding platforms and hallways, punctuated by strong smells of urine, feces, and disease;

(5) an increase in loud, boisterous, crazy, and violent mental patients and homeless people screaming at no one in particular, but menacing and harassing the various passengers in NYC's transit system, making a routine subway ride now a life-threatening and dangerous risk;

(6) routine stops midway between station stops, with thousands of people trapped underground in spots with no internet, no air, no ventilation, and no one to help, compounded with extreme crowding to the point where one seriously questions if they will actually survive the trip—many people with anxiety issues find this development to be

the most disturbing and life-threatening, with their blood pressure, pulses, heart rate, and body heat increasing to the point of panic;

(7) big, fat, dirty, hairy rats carrying various diseases in full bloom, reproducing profusely, trampling through the railway tracks and up and around the platform, daring humans to challenge them;

(8) sporadic murders with people being shoved off the platforms reaching an all-time high, as the lunatic asylums of NYC are prematurely emptied of their occupants, seemingly given directions to head directly to the NYC MTA subway system;

(9) extremely hot platform areas during the hottest day of summer, leaving people covered in sweat streaming from their faces and bodies, drenching their clothes all the way through, and suffering from near-tundra-like conditions in the dead of winter;

(10) the walls and infrastructure of the subway system falling apart, dilapidated, and dreary, with bricks coming off and wall plaster peeling everywhere, with all the surface areas badly needing paint or some other type of cosmetic cover-up, all of which only add to the extremely depressing and disgusting status of the NYC subway system.

It has not been this bad in decades. Indeed during Mayor Rudolph Giuliani and then-mayor Michael Bloomberg's stints for nearly two decades, the subway system was the crown and jewel of mass transit, and it was rumored that Mayor Bloomberg even traveled the subway every morning to get to work.

Clearly if Michael Bloomberg was riding the subway regularly as mayor, he was not going to tolerate the above-listed conditions at all, and he did something about them all to make sure that they were fixed and dealt with.

That was a real leader.

And Mayor Giuliani was equally concerned with the status of the subways and also flexed his muscles and clenched his fists in true leadership form and snapped it all into shape, after the disastrous tenures of Mayor David Dinkins and Mayor Koch before him.

New York City desperately needs a mayor who will address these issues, but it appears that Joe Lhota, currently head of the MTA Subway System, doesn't really like Democrat Mayor Bill de Blasio that much, possibly because Lhota is a Republican having formerly worked for the Rudy Giuliani administration and knows that making the vast majority of NYC's residents and inhabitants dread and detest the subway system is the most visible, easy, and glaring way of ensuring that they vote him out of office.

It appears that either Mayor de Blasio does not have enough control over NYC's subway system, or Joe Lhota is deliberately messing around with it, instructing his staff from the top on down to either exacerbate the above-listed horrific conditions of the NYC Subway system, or is preventing de Blasio from dealing with it himself.

Either way, whoever is responsible for this needs to be fired immediately and possibly prosecuted, just as Governor Chris Christie's staff was targeted after it was revealed that they may have deliberately tampered with the traffic on the George Washington Bridge to punish another politician, Mark Sokolich, in the Fort Lee, New Jersey, area for not towing the line politically, thus ruining and destroying the commute of hundreds of millions of people trying to get back and forth for work and life.

In that case, the United States attorney for the District of New Jersey, Paul J. Fishman, launched a massive federal investigation, resulting in a sweeping nine-count indictment against Bridget Anne Kelly, the deputy chief of staff, Baroni, and Wildstein.

Wildstein entered a guilty plea and testified against Baroni and Kelly, who were found guilty on all counts in November 2016.

David Samson pleaded guilty to one felony count of conspiracy in July 2016, for acts unrelated to the lane closures but unearthed by the federal Bridgegate investigation.

A real leader needs to be installed either as head of the MTA Subway System or in the mayor's office, and a criminal investigation needs to be opened up by the New York FBI as well as the US attorneys in the Southern and Eastern Districts of New York.

The people of NYC deserve much better, and it won't do anymore for these two idiots to keep blaming each other, pointing their fingers at each other, while eight million New Yorkers and hundreds of millions of tourists from all over the world suffer in extreme squalor.

If US Pulls Out/Violates Iran Nuclear Deal, then No Nation Could (Or Should) Trust US Diplomacy

Some international treaties are more important than others.

Pulling out of the Paris Climate Agreement or the Trans-Pacific Partnership international treaties by President Donald Trump was no big deal, relatively, because no one was in any real or immediate danger of dying because of it, regardless of what the alarmist climate progressives or international globalist corporations may have screamed about.

If anything, pulling out of those agreements could merely be seen as a regrouping effort by the United States, in order to once again find its sea legs and reboot before going back full blown into the world of international commerce, trade, governance, or relationships.

But pulling out of, or otherwise violating, the Joint Comprehensive Plan of Action (otherwise known as the JCPOA or Iran Nuclear Deal) would be a monumentally huge and stupid thing to do, considering what is on the line in doing so.

Right now the only result of outright international warfare, resulting in the drawing in of massive continents and subcontinents, as well as technologically sophisticated nations, would inevitably lead directly to nuclear war, in other words, the end of humanity.

In that case, people would die, billions of people exactly, if not the entire global population now approaching nine billion souls internationally.

This is not a risk anyone should take, and the JCPOA, negotiated by the P5+1 nations (China, France, Russia, the United Kingdom, and the United States, plus Germany) with the US being represented under the President Barack Obama administration by Secretary of State John Kerry, represented one of the greatest diplomatic achievements in human history in order to avoid World War III and restore balance and peace to the force.

Respecting the JCPOA deal should be of paramount importance to all the world's leaders, not just the ones being restricted.

To that end, if North Korea's Kim Jong-un ever decided to approach the negotiating table at the multiple requests of South Korea's President Moon Jaein, and countless other world leaders, including President Donald Trump's cabinet members and staff such as Defense Secretary James "Mad Dog" Mattis and Secretary of State Rex Tillerson, then the USA needs to be able to stand straight up, look at the North Korean leader and his staff straight in the eye, and say with total confidence, "You can trust us."

Otherwise the US's word is as good as a pile of dog refuse, and no one would ever enter into an international treaty or agreement voluntarily, giving up their nuclear/biological/chemical stockpiles, ever again, and they would have every reason not to.

There is no wiggle room on this one. The Iran Nuclear Deal managed to single-handedly disarm the nuclear ambitions and progress of the Iranian government without firing a shot, and if smarter cooler heads prevail, perhaps the US can now follow suit and eventually do trillions of dollars of business with them, just like the Europeans are starting and trying to currently do.

At the end of the day, the USA needs to remember the wise words of one of its greatest founding fathers, Thomas Jefferson, when he declared, "Peace, commerce and honest friendship with all nations; entangling alliances with none."

Because the only thing that really protects and safeguards different nations from attacking or being attacked by other nations is when their mutual business relationships and monetary/financial/economic health are hopelessly bound together, just like the air that we breath and the planet that we share.

Netanyahu Needs to Publicly/Officially Condemn Discrimination for His Own Legacy and Israel's

Benjamin Netanyahu needs to publicly and officially establish Israel's policies on state-sanctioned discrimination, or he will not only destroy his own legacy, but he will drag Israel into the abyss with him.

Jewish people all around the world like to celebrate and extol that they are often at the forefront of civil rights, human rights, progressivism, and human evolution when it comes to pushing the human race forward in terms of viewpoints on race, sexual orientation, religion, ethnicity, national origin, and skin color.

But for some reason, Israel was founded by well-known and rabid racists, sexists, and men who openly espoused and propagated the most barbaric and crude personal beliefs and sentiments on all of the above issues, such as David Ben Gurion.

And it is only getting worse under the Netanyahu presidency.

Billions of social media users all across the world, whether it is through Facebook or Twitter or other mechanisms, are treated to an almost daily regimen of videos and photographs of state-sanctioned violence, racism, discrimination, bullying, and apartheid by Israeli police, military, government officials, and citizens against seemingly and relatively powerless people, and it is making the world collectively sick to their stomach to see this, even though the Israeli government under Netanyahu is openly and aggressively working with and collaborating with these social media companies to stifle and censor such news.

It is no longer acceptable or believable for Netanyahu and his ilk to proclaim that this is being done for the sake of Israeli security and safety, that they are at war with Islamic fundamentalism, because only last week the State of Israel also placed a formal and permanent ban on gay marriage—and this also indicates Israel's strong move to a normalized status of hatred, exclusion, and state-sanctioned discrimination of all people not created in Netanyahu or his oligarchy backers' likeness.

Israel is also engaging in increased, augmented, open, and abject discrimination against women and even internally against different populations of their own Israeli Jews, based on race, skin color, ethnicity, and national origin.

How can depriving its own Jewish people who differ with regards to race, sexual orientation, religious differences, skin color, and national origin help Israeli security?

The fact is, it doesn't.

With these new policy moves Israel under Netanyahu has openly revealed his viewpoints and those of his most vocal and cash-rich supporters.

If Israel truly wants to fulfill its stated objective of being a beacon of light unto the nations, then it needs to quickly and unequivocally condemn officially all acts and patterns of discrimination, if not for Benjamin Netanyahu's own legacy, then for Israel's.

The fact remains that there are 198 nations within the United Nations, and the vast majority are nonwhite, and an even larger majority are non-Jewish.

To that end, with Israel offending and insulting each and every single other nation on planet earth, this is resulting in a self-fulfilling prophecy, creating a slow, agonizing, inevitable destruction and state suicide.

Unless a government is bought and paid for with its leadership and oligarchy class by Israel's oligarch supporters/backers, that nation will openly condemn and detest the State of Israel and Netanyahu under the Likud party, because Israel and Netanyahu hated and discriminated against them, and their people, first.

One must seriously question the sanity and long-term strategy of President Benjamin Netanyahu for not seeing the hugely problematic public relations nightmare that he has caused for Israel and his own government, fanning the flames to make it even worse.

It is not just the Palestinian Arab Muslims that he and Israel are crushing under the wheels of their tanks anymore, or whose houses they are firebombing, or schools they are destroying, or drinking water they are cutting off or polluting. It is now also apparently anyone who does not fit within the racial, ethnic, skin color, sexual orientation, national origin or even sect of Judaism that Benjamin Netanyahu and the oligarchy class of Israeli leadership and corporate/banking powers that they belong to.

And in this way, he has ensured that Israel will implode from the inside, rather than from any real (or imagined) powers from outside of it.

And this is truly a sad development.

The only question that remains is whether or not this is accidentally happening, or is this being done purposefully, and who is driving this suicide mission of pushing Israel (and Netanyahu) off the proverbial cliff?

Cooperation, Not Sanctions, Will Make America Great Again

Someone needs to tell President Donald Trump that his own US Treasury Department chief, Steve Mnuchin, mass purveyor of reckless and shortsighted economic trade sanctions, is undermining his ability to truly make America great again.

While the rest of the world trades freely, now in multiple currencies, the constant bullying, threats, and intimidation by the Neocons begging for more violent and destructive foreign interventions, resulting in countless millions dead all over the world, sovereign nations ruined, and new state-led enemies vowing to destroy America for ending their existence, the United States is becoming more and more isolated, hated, and reviled, while its people and small businesses get choked to death because they can no longer trade with the new, countless, and ever-growing list of enemies.

This is all the while the major international corporations and banks, who have absolutely no loyalty to the USA, continue to trade freely, avoiding these proverbial sanctions by merely bypassing international laws and restrictions, changing corporate forms and home state identities to continue on, business as usual.

Much like the crazed, misguided Neocons who have physically destroyed or infiltrated foreign governments, arming/backing open terrorist groups to kill off other countries, the US Treasury Neocons are using the power of the international purse to further this agenda of ruining other nations economically, while also at the same time making middle Americans hated and their small businesses being driven into bankruptcy and destruction, not even being able to safely travel out of their own borders anymore.

Again, these flyover Americans within the US government watch with wry smiles as their fellow countrymen are being destroyed and plundered with the ad hoc, flippant rules that they create, while continuing on making even more money than before, by having one foot within the international corporate and banking structures, owing no allegiance whatsoever to America.

Now, with the latest idiotic and foolhardy development of Steve Mnuchin cutting out the People's Republic of China out of the American sphere of trade influence, coming quickly on the heels of cutting out Russia and Iran, these latter two nations heavily involved in the burgeoning, extremely wealthy, and cash/resource rich trade zone of Eurasia, the USA might as well declare bankruptcy now and dissolve its founding documents and constitution.

The only nations in the world that benefit now are the ones that jump ship and abandon the US petrodollar because they quite simply have to survive, feed their people, and maintain their national infrastructure.

The unilateral actions of the US Treasury Department have now forced the economic unification of the greatest competing economic powers in the world, namely, Russia, China, Iran, and other oil/gas/resource rich nations in order to survive, grow, and prosper.

Now even small nations like Venezuela are finding the balls to dump the US dollar because they know that they will be quickly scooped up by these BRICS nations in a heartbeat for trade, loans, project finance, and even defense cooperation.

The lunatics are clearly in charge of the nut house in the US government, and it would be hilarious if it did not inevitably wind up in the end of America.

Cooperation and diplomacy is the key to international success and making America great again, not folding up into a fetal position and sucking our proverbial thumb in the corner, wailing and crying in a temper tantrum while the international adults in the room continue to play and trade and work together for a better world.

As Adam Garrie of the *Duran* newspaper writes in his seminal article "China Helps Venezuela and Iran against Unilateral US Sanctions: China Walks through the Doors the US Has Left Wide Open," the writing is unfortunately already on the wall.

The USA needs to pull up its international economic/trade proverbial airplane before it crashes into the equally metaphoric mountain of existential ruin.

It's Time to Ban Automatic Weapons of Any Kind from High Population Density Areas

Even vociferous supporters of the Second Amendment to the US Constitution, including undersigned, no longer have an argument against an outright and blanket ban of any and all automatic weapons from high population density areas of the United States of America any longer after the horrific and inexplicable largest mass shooting in US history in Las Vegas during the month of October 2017.

If one lone nut such as uber-vanilla Steven Paddock can take out thousands of innocent people murdering hundreds in his wake, then something drastic needs to be done, because this will only be the beginning by terrorists both domestic and foreign.

Conspiracy theorists be damned because the American people will still be able to own and sell automatic weapons in low-density-population areas of the United States, thus protecting their much-prized militia movement to safeguard their freedoms from new world order types and globalists looking to grab their guns.

There are mechanisms that could theoretically strike a balance by and between the US Constitution Second Amendment and Public Safety, however, and they need to be explored:

1) Most civilized nations throughout the world have mandatory and perfunctory metal detector apparatus systems at all entryways into their facilities if they are close to high population density locations within their major cities.

2) There should no longer be a distinction between semiautomatic versus automatic and assault weapons since these weapons can be easily altered/converted into one or another.

3) Life sentences should be handed down if one is found to be trafficking / selling / in possession of an automatic weapon in high population density areas.

4) Specific federal lawsuit legislation, criminal penalties, and legal causes of action should be enacted by Congress and the Senate against any and all facilities and executives (hotels, stadiums, etc.) that have been found to have either housed or enabled sick demented killers like Steven Paddock from storing weapons or launching their mass killings, as well as similar penalties for immediate family members or friends who

maybe have been aware of said planning or proclivity, in order to help bankrupt those entities which made it easier for these fiends to commit their crimes. This will undoubtedly help increase private security and reporting mechanisms in order to protect themselves from mass lawsuits, incarceration, and financial ruin.

5) Outright ban on automatic weapons sales at gun shows and other informal marketplaces and venues.

6) Automatic weapon registration with local, state, and federal law enforcement agencies in all fifty states, including where automatic weapons possession/sales are banned.

7) Limiting of all automatic weapons sales by US and foreign manufacturers only to the US military and US government, including police and federal law enforcement.

8) Increase in automatic weapon detection apparatus and technology to sniff out any and all automatic weapons by law enforcement in the midst of any high population density community or population.

9) New federal legislation against weapons manufacturers and sellers when their weaponry is found to have been used in a mass shooting, similar to the ITAR and AECA rules promulgated by the US State Department punishing anyone (brokers, dealers, sellers, manufacturers) who was linked to weapons falling into the hands of international terrorist end users, regardless of whether or not their initial customers were law abiding individuals/entities.

10) Enlist gun rights lobbyists such as the NRA to help create, draft, and enact said legislation so that it gets an official seal of approval from any potential enemies of these protective mechanisms.

The above are just some of the measures to ensure not only that no more mass shootings take place in the USA but that also satisfy gun enthusiasts and proponents of the Second Amendment to help protect and safeguard people in their homes and their freedom from enemies, both foreign and domestic.

Decertifying Iran Nuclear Deal Would Ultimately Be Bad for Both USA and Israel

While President Donald Trump is very fond of proclaiming that the Iran Nuclear Deal was an embarrassment and a horrible deal, he neglects to remember that the USA was not the only party to this deal and, in fact, was literally forced to the table by the P5+1 nations, which included Germany, Russia, the United Kingdom, China, and France, in the face of great opposition by the huge money and lobbying powers of Saudi Arabia, Israel, and the Neoconservatives in the United States.

But the deal makes sense because it diplomatically and without firing a single shot managed to disarm the Iranian government for the foreseeable future of nuclear weaponry while jump-starting diplomatic, defense, and trade relations by and between this formally isolated nation of Iran and all the aforementioned countries above in terms of trade and defense ties, all of which lead to global peace, stability, and prosperity.

The deal also allowed for unprecedented access for inspection any and all corners of Iran by outside entities to ensure that they were not developing weapons of mass destruction as well.

All too often, President Trump and the desperate members of the organized and well-funded opposition to the Iran Nuclear Deal forget that Iran is a bona fide enemy of the ISIS terrorist group (or maybe they don't since they created/funded/armed them), which was funded, trained, armed, and facilitated by the Saudi, Neocon, European, and Israeli fringe groups in their intelligence and business circles, who quite frankly are the international super oligarchs who formerly controlled 99 percent of the world's wealth and military power, but whose wealth, money, and power are waning daily with the rise of the great consolidated powers of the East.

This small international oligarch group of people care little about the vast population of the globe, almost eight billion people, and once they eliminate all their opposition in the world, they would have no use left for any of them, and mass depopulation would most probably ensue.

See Henry Kissinger's National Security Memo 200 for further guidance on this issue.

The only ones standing in their way of complete and total unbridled power, militarily and financially, are the very bloc that is forming right before our eyes in the East, and decertifying the Iran nuclear deal would only push all of them closer in terms of defense and trade ties, i.e., China, Russia, Iran, Eurasia, Europe, and now latecomer and former NATO ally, Turkey.

These entities know far too well that it is in their best interests to stick together, and work together, rather than continue to be a client state of the USA, Saudi Arabia, and Israel.

Pulling out or decertifying the Iran Nuclear Deal will also have the unfortunate effect of causing every single nation in the world to never trust US Diplomacy again, and they would never enter into another defense or trade agreement with the US to disarm, because they know that it would never be upheld.

Hence the only way the US and global community would ever get North Korea to disarm and abandon their nuclear program would be through outright war, terrorism, and death (and many tens millions of Americans would die as well, if not completely obliterated).

While the Iran Nuclear Agreement was not perfect by any stretch of the imagination in terms of US and Israeli interests 100 percent, compromise is always part of a deal.

But at least the US, Israel, and global community know that Iran will not have nuclear, chemical, or biological weapons anytime soon, and this could also, if played correctly, by an open door to extremely lucrative and mutually beneficial defense and trade ties, which would make everyone money, and feel secure in their homes, rather than decertifying the deal and placing them on a fast horse toward becoming a full-blown nuclear/chemical/biological weapons state that doesn't do business with either the US, Israel, or Saudi Arabia at all, merely forcing them to be in the camp of Eurasia, China, Russia, Turkey, Europe, and beyond.

The periodic temper tantrums of President Donald Trump are now causing a rift in his own national security team, including Defense Secretary James "Mad Dog" Mattis, Secretary of State Rex Tillerson, National Security Advisor H. R. McMaster, and plenty of others.

The Iran Nuclear Deal is also wholeheartedly supported by a huge swath of patriotic and risk-averse career intelligence and defense officials within the State of Israel itself, within its Mossad, Shin Bet, and government (if not already pushed out by Netanyahu).

Only Trump and Netanyahu are screaming all by themselves on their mountain tops.

The fact remains that the only ones who would benefit from the US decertifying / pulling out of the Iran Nuclear Deal would be the international bankers and corporations and flyover, wealthy oligarch Americans, Israelis, and Saudis, who all owe no loyalty or allegiance to any of their home nations or people, and will make a financial killing in the new and burgeoning oil and gas industries emanating out of the Silk Road of China, surrounded by Russia, Iran, Turkey, Eurasia, Kazakhstan, Turkmenistan, Uzbekistan, and ironically enough, Europe.

Meanwhile the people of the USA and Israel will be isolated like no other time in their history, unable to have defense or trade ties with any of these nations, all the while the Saudi petrodollar continues to tank, with their country and nation teetering on the brink of existential abyss, because you simply cannot have three thousand family members completely control and oppress thirty-three million angry, poverty-stricken people in the year 2017.

The USA needs to replenish itself in the waters of one of its greatest founding fathers, Thomas Jefferson, and remember his statement of "peace, commerce and honest friendship with all nations, entangling alliances with none."

At least in theory.

Otherwise, the USA and Israel will just go the way of the Nazis—hated, reviled, isolated, attacked, and ultimately, extinct.

Can Europe Save America from Google?

P resident Donald Trump has apparently appointed Joseph Simons and Rohit Chopra to run the Antitrust Division at the Federal Trade Commission (FTC).

It was allegedly proven by Julian Assange's WikiLeaks and multiple other sources that Google deliberately screwed Donald Trump over during his campaign by showcasing and highlighting negative attacks on his reputation and campaign, while hiding and obfuscating negative publicity and search engine terminology against Hillary Clinton.

But because the incoming Trump Federal Trade Commission (FTC) was about to retain Joshua Wright, a former Google-friendly FTC crony, similar to the Goldman Sachs model of high-level crime enjoying a revolving door with the US Treasury and Federal Reserve with its executives Robert Rubin, Larry Summers, Hank Paulson, Tim Geithner, and Gene Sperling (who all engineered the 2008 financial crisis), it appears that the United States of America is truly being held captive by both Google and Goldman Sachs, with both its outgoing (and incoming) government being held ransom by these two corporate/finance/technology behemoths.

Currently, however, the European Union led by heroic Antitrust investigator Margrethe Vestager is going after Google big-time, having already sanctioned them to the tune of three billion dollars, with Russia, South Korea, France, and other countries already having beaten the stuffing out of Google with multiple judgments against them for antitrust activity, unfair and deceptive business practices, abuse of monopoly power, search engine manipulation for political/financial reasons, tax evasion, government corruption and interference, and other criminal acts and antics.

Even though Donald Trump publicly stated that he would strengthen the FTC in order to block the upcoming scary AT&T–Time Warner merger, he has apparently abandoned that idea, and it also seems that he doesn't care very much about Google's awesome but threatening power, even though their full force, political might, corruption, cronyism with the Obama White House, ties to Hillary Clinton and the Deep State plutocrat elite, trillions of dollars, lobbying power, and overall octopus-like tentacles tried to destroy and derail his campaign first.

Maybe Donald Trump now realizes that he will have to accommodate Google in order to get his agenda passed, even though he has indicated that he doesn't like to capitulate to the Deep State powers that be.

Therefore, it appears that the future of the world and its freedom lies in the hands of the European Union. Can its Antitrust investigation of Google liberate America from the yoke of slavery under Google and its control of the United States government?

Unelected, Unappointed Court Magistrates/Law Clerks/Staff Undermine US Judiciary Third Branch of Government

Most Americans are aware that there are three branches in the US government: the legislative, the executive, and the judiciary.

Those same Americans have also heard that the legislative and executive branches are completely and totally vulnerable to outside money powers and lobbying groups that actively seek to undercut the wishes and will of the average American voter by sponsoring and essentially bribing the two former-named bodies of American government in order to get what they want within US domestic and foreign policy.

However, few Americans are able to grasp the concept that the American judiciary (federal, state, and local) are also equally susceptible to this type of bribery, lobbying, and institutionalized corruption through their Achilles' heel —the unelected, unappointed, and generally life-serving court magistrates, law clerks, and administrative staff that heavily populate and run the American judicial system.

These court officers and staff literally run amok in America's courts, issuing decisions and deciding what happens to lawyers and litigants each and every day, with little to no scrutiny paid to them, their daily activities, who they know and talk to, and who they get bribed / paid by, in order to affect and influence case outcomes and decisions.

Nearly all the fifty states in America have some type of commission on judicial conduct, where supposedly average American citizens can file complaints against corrupt judges who routinely flout the law, violate administrative and judicial (substantive and procedural) due process, and who otherwise act and engage in conduct and behavior which smacks loudly of corruption, cronyism, and the fundamental deprivation of civil rights and liberties, all under the color of law and authority.

But these same state commissions on judicial conduct are notorious for routinely rubber stamping form dismissal letters of these citizen complaints, no matter how serious the allegations or well-documented with tangible evidence of misconduct / evidence tampering / obstruction of justice / denial of due process that they are, because these commissions will often state that they do not have jurisdiction over magistrates, law clerks, and court staff because those individuals are not judges and thereby fall out of the paradigm of what they were constituted by the American citizenry to address.

Herein lies the rub—and herein lies the secret back door for organized crime, foreign and domestic intelligence services, private investigators, criminals, and other organized (or disorganized) corrupting elements to do their dirty work.

Routinely, and seemingly daily, these out-of-control, unregulated, and unsupervised court magistrates, law clerks, and court administrative staff that infest our nation's federal, state, local, family, civil, and criminal courts will

(1) lose your motion papers;

(2) alter your motion papers;

(3) remove or tamper with evidence;

(4) write court decisions without the knowledge or permission of their judge bosses, and then get them signed off surreptitiously under the judge's name;

(5) take money bribes, pecuniary promises, make side deals, and meet with people or individuals representing opposing sides in an illegal and unethical fashion, in order to affect or influence the case outcome;

(6) engage in improper and illicit sexual relationships with litigants, their children or family members, and lawyers to influence case decisions and outcomes;

(7) hide important information from judges;

(8) retaliate against disfavored or unpopular (or less monied) litigants/lawyers who complain about, or challenge, them;

(9) delay or derail court dates, proceedings, and hearings; and

(10) all in all completely undermine and pollute the third and arguably most important branch of the United States government, all under the watchful eye of the government.

Thus, it is no surprise when the Federal Bureau of Investigation (which has been accused of collaborating with these court parasites under their outlawed COINTELPRO, now called COPS, program to target/retaliate against certain disfavored lawyers/litigants) routinely tell American citizen complainants that they cannot investigate or open up a complaint when obvious judicial corruption or misconduct exists because they quite simply have no jurisdiction over judges, who are supposed to be neutral and impartial arbiters of American justice under the color of law and authority.

Similarly, other law enforcement and regulatory agencies of the US government also routinely tell American citizen complainants that there is nothing that they can do when confronted with these types of legal abuses emanating from the federal, state, and local government in this third judicial branch because, again, "they do not have jurisdiction."

Unfortunately today, this means that well-funded and well-organized criminal groups, organizations, movements, foreign and domestic intelligence agencies, terrorists, and other monied enemies of the American government and its people are also aware of this and take full advantage of this weakness to exploit it for their own political and financial gain.

This is why horrific groups and organizations seem to keep getting away with their crimes in broad and open daylight, such as global and domestic child pornographers and pedophile child traffickers, illegal and illicit drug traffickers and narcotics purveyors, organized crime, terrorists, illegal arms/weapons traffickers and gun runners, illegal alien smuggling rings, coyotes, and other human slave traffickers, and other well-funded, billion-dollar illegal entities.

The American people need to realize and recognize that organized judicial corruption and misconduct is indeed a multivariate national security risk and problem as it helps judges avoid accountability and responsibility and keeps the trillion-dollar organized criminal, terrorist, and espionage groups around the world in thriving and expanding business, all at the expense of the average American citizen, voter, and taxpayer.

And it is now high time for this type of organized and institutionalized form of government corruption to end, and end now.

The American people need to demand that these unelected, unappointed, life-serving, and thoroughly corrupted court magistrates, law clerks, and court administrative staff be subject to the same (if not more) scrutiny, regulation, discipline, supervision, and monitoring that their judge bosses seem to be put through for the sake of the United States of America and its national security and day-to-day integrity.

President Trump Should Declare National Emergency to Defeat Communists Infiltrating US Government

The Constitution does not expressly grant the president additional powers in times of national emergency.

However, many scholars think that the framers implied these powers because the structural design of the executive branch enables it to act much faster than the legislative branch.

Unfortunately, the international-banker-controlled, Neoconservative/Neoliberal, Leftist, Communist infiltration of the United States legislature (Congress/Senate) and the federal/state judiciary is complete, rendering the ability of President Donald Trump to lead and carry out the will of the American people impossible as head of the third executive branch.

This was precisely the fear of Federal Bureau of Investigation director and founder J. Edgar Hoover, but it unfortunately came true after his death in 1972.

After the former communist Soviet Union was dissolved in 1991, the international bankers controlling communism instead focused on controlling and infiltrating the United States of America and its government.

This was made a whole lot easier after the US Supreme Court case *Citizens United v. FEC* allowed them to purchase each and every elected American government official with ease, even if entire communities of US citizens opposed them.

Currently in the US, gridlock remains the rule of the land, and even time sensitive and desperate issues like lowering the astronomical cost of Obamacare from its enormous unaffordable premiums for the American people cannot get rectified.

National Emergency Declaration

A claim of emergency powers was at the center of President Abraham Lincoln's suspension of habeas corpus without Congressional approval in 1861.

Lincoln claimed that the rebellion created an emergency that permitted him the extraordinary power of unilaterally suspending the writ.

With Chief Justice Roger Taney sitting as judge, the Federal District Court of Maryland struck down the suspension in Ex parte Merryman, although Lincoln ignored the order. (Greenberg, David, "Lincoln's Crackdown," Slate).

Herein lies the case and historical precedent for President Donald Trump to save the American republic from the civil war existing by and between the America-firsters and the foreign globalist communist elements trying to derail the United States and force it to be subjugated into the international community without the rights and privileges accompanying US citizenship.

A linear succession of global internationalist Communists have led the United States in the Office of the Presidency for nearly the past thirty years, and their coordinated work against the interests of the American people is now nearly complete. Each and every day, President Donald Trump is running into oligarch-built road blocks and political glass ceilings designed to prevent him from delivering for the American people, and a full-blown Communist rebellion has now fully taken afoot in retaliation for his successful election by the American people.

This Communist rebellion has come in the forms of the ludicrous Russia Collusion hearings in both the US Congress and Senate, being propped up nonstop 24-7 by the mainstream media and being spearheaded by Special Counsel Robert Mueller, a suspected leader and proponent of these international globalist communist infiltrators.

Many argue that Robert Mueller is merely taking revenge for the firing of James Comey, former FBI chief, who is also equally entrenched in the international banker communist conspiracy, having tasted it while working on the board of directors of London-based HSBC Bank after serving as US attorney for the Southern District of New York.

President Theodore Roosevelt famously called the presidency a bully pulpit from which to raise issues nationally, because when a president raises an issue, it inevitably becomes subject to public debate.

President Donald Trump has successfully used his Twitter account and other social media outlets to raise issues important to the American people, as well as speak directly to them, in defiance of the mainstream media, which is nearly 100 percent controlled by the international banks and global communists.

A president's power and influence may be limited, but politically the president is certainly the most important power in Washington, DC, and furthermore is one of the most famous and influential of all Americans.

Within the executive branch itself, the president has broad powers to manage national affairs and the priorities of the government.

The president can issue rules, regulations, and instructions called executive orders, which have the binding force of law upon federal agencies but do not require approval of the United States Congress.

Executive orders are subject to judicial review and interpretation, however, but this is after the fact.

The president, as the commander in chief of the United States Armed

Forces, may also call into federal service individual state units of the National Guard.

In times of war or national emergency, the Congress has already granted the president broader powers to manage the national economy and protect the security of the United States. ("Executive Power," Legal Information Institute, Cornell University Law School).

A state of emergency is a situation in which a government is empowered to perform actions that it would normally not be allowed to.

A government can declare such a state of emergency during a disaster, civil unrest, or armed conflict.

National Emergencies Act

The National Emergencies Act regulates this process at the federal level.

It requires the president to specifically identify the provisions activated and to renew the declaration annually, so as to prevent an arbitrarily broad or open-ended emergency.

Presidents have occasionally taken action justified as necessary or prudent because of a state of emergency, subject to review by the courts, but again, after the fact *(Youngstown Sheet and Tube Co. v. Sawyer, 1953)*.

The act authorizes the president to activate emergency provisions of law via an emergency declaration, on the condition that the president specifies the provisions so activated and notifies Congress.

An activation would expire if the president expressly terminated the emergency, or did not renew the emergency annually, or if each house of Congress passed a resolution terminating the emergency.

After presidents objected to this Congressional termination provision on separation of powers grounds, it was replaced in 1985 with termination by an enacted joint resolution.

The act also requires that the president and executive agencies maintain records of all orders and regulations that proceed from the use of emergency authority and to regularly report the cost incurred to Congress.

Unitary Executive Theory

The unitary executive theory is a theory of American constitutional law holding that the president possesses the power to control the entire executive branch.

The doctrine is rooted in Article II of the United States Constitution, which vests "the executive power" of the United States in the president.

The vesting clause of Article II provides, "The executive power [of the United States] shall be vested in a President of the United States of America."

Proponents of the unitary executive theory argue that this language, along with the Take Care Clause ("The President shall *take care* that the laws be faithfully executed") creates a "hierarchical, unified executive department under the direct control of the President" *(The Structural Constitution: Unitary Executive, Plural Judiciary,* Harvard Law Review, 105 [6]).

In its most extreme form, unitary executive theory can mean that neither Congress nor the federal courts can tell the president what to do, or how to do it, particularly regarding national security matters (Dean, John [2007], *Broken Government,* Viking. p. 102. ISBN 9780670018208).

National Security and Homeland Security Presidential Directive

The National Security and Homeland Security Presidential Directive says that when the president considers a national emergency to have occurred, an Enduring Constitutional Government, comprising "a cooperative effort among the executive, legislative, and judicial branches of the Federal Government, coordinated by the President," will take the place of the nation's regular government.

This clearly places the president in his executive capacity to be above the other two branches, legislative and judiciary, to "coordinate" the "comity" by and between all three branches during a declaration of this national security emergency.

This presidential directive was signed into law by President George W. Bush on May 4, 2007, which claims the power to execute procedures for continuity of the federal government in the event of a catastrophic emergency, such as "any incident, regardless of location, that results in extraordinary levels of mass casualties, damage, or disruption severely affecting the U.S. population, infrastructure, environment, economy, or government functions."

This condition would be very easy for President Donald Trump to satisfy, given the current circumstances of the US economy, extreme corruption/government gridlock, and Communist infiltration of the US government in its current form.

The signing of this directive was not surprisingly not covered by the mainstream US media, or discussed by the US Congress.

Since President Donald Trump has already declared a national emergency with respect to the opioid crisis, even his own administration has case precedent to get this done on an immediate and urgent basis.

Climate Change Is Apparently
Only a Problem if You Travel Overseas

To most Americans, climate change and horrible air pollution is a myth, a mere conspiracy theory wherein the globalists and the oligarchs of the world are trying to enact global treaties for carbon emission taxation and penalties designed to usher in a global new world order government.

This was the main reason the American people really did not shed a tear or even whimper when the United States recently left the Paris Climate Accord Treaty, which was under the purview of the United Nations Framework Convention on Climate Change (UNFCCC), dealing with greenhouse gas emissions mitigation, adaptation, and finance starting in the year 2020.

However, there was a major point to President Donald Trump's decision to leave this agreement on or about June 2017 because, by and large, the United States is a safe and healthy haven for climate control and emissions standards thanks to the wonderful work of the Environmental Protection Agency (EPA) and other heroic federal, state, and local agencies designed to monitor and keep under control greenhouse gas and carbon emissions to keep America's air as pure as possible.

So to that end, because the US is a very responsible and self-monitoring nation, its carbon emission is actually very much under control, and it is not a pressing matter as other issues seem to be.

Added to the mix is the fact that the major carbon emitter nations are third and second world countries who desperately care more about their rapid economic growth rather than the long-term ill effects on the health of their people. The American people are even more far removed from this pressing issue of the day, because, quite frankly, they don't really see or experience it on a daily basis.

However, the real pivotal issue is this: unless the typical American (or even European, South American, or African) visits and actually sees, breaths, and experiences the literal toxic waste dump that is the surrounding air situation in China and India, the globe's greatest, largest, and most egregious offenders, one has absolutely no idea how dire the situation actually is.

Because when one steps off the airplane in either India or China, one is immediately hit by a wall of pea-soup-like, thick, horrific mass of white, brown, viscous, and oppressive smog of carbon-based particulates and dirt right in the face, and the assault on one's lungs begins.

Over the month of November 2017, when US President Donald Trump visited Asia, there were reports emanating out of India and China that showed that their people literally could not even see their hands before their eyes and wherein the air quality was tantamount to smoking fifty cigarettes per day, and where India was even forced to implement near-martial law by ordering all automobiles off the road on alternate days, and also ordering farmers to cease and desist from mass burnings of their agricultural fields after their harvests, which were causing massive eruptions and belchings of carbon-based toxic emissions and thick black smoke into the air, rising high into the atmosphere above the Himalayan mountains and even comingling with China's already-heavy carbon-based emissions to literally blind and choke off the populations of both nations, each having more than one billion people, and covering a massive part of the earth's land mass.

Empirical data and studies were showing that the acceptable carbon emissions were being blown away by sometimes as high as seven to eight hundred times the normal rate in the incredibly dangerous phase, and people literally could not see their own hands in front of their own faces.

How this massive, earth-shattering problem manages to escape the American psyche is truly a gargantuan problem, because the Americans lead the way in terms of global governance, international treaties, and world consciousness about problems that require fixing.

If the USA pulls out or loses interest in certain topics, then for some reason, that topic/issue dies a slow, painful death, doomed to the realm of obscurity, and forgotten forever.

The problem is that air quality is a global phenomenon, and bad, dirty, carbon-filled air and smog travel all around the world and is not confined to just the Americas.

The slow-encapsulating black death of dangerously high carbon emissions and chokingly bad air quality are enveloping the United States like a frog sitting in slowly heated and then boiling water, wherein the proverbial frog is dead before he even knows it.

While Americans generally stare up at blue skies and bask in the glory of the relatively clean utopian American ecosystem thanks to the heroic and timeless work of the EPA and other agencies, they remain completely and totally oblivious to the slow, creeping, imminent, and impending black death approaching their shores in the form of hellish carbon emissions coming over from Asia.

To that extent, it was quite understandable when President Donald Trump encountered little to no resistance when he announced his pullout from the aforementioned international climate treaty, because Americans don't really see this problem in front of their faces.

But Americans must understand and internalize that this issue is now only a few days/weeks/years away from permanent damage not only to the world's resources, wildlife, fisheries, trees, and land masses but also is directly responsible for human ills such as cancer, birth defects, shortened life spans, infant mortality, heart and lung disease, emotional and mental problems, and numerous countless health concerns and problems that will be impossible to reverse or fix.

It is vitally important that Americans both read and educate themselves more about this, if not travel more, because the clock is literally ticking away to the point of irreversible death and destruction, when even the EPA and America's geographical isolation from the rest of the world will no longer be able to either save us or allow us to remain in our collective state of delusional self-denial about what is actually happening and going on in this world.

Trading Places China and the United States Need to Work Together to Forge a Better World

T he story of the Chinese economy is truly miraculous—how this nation of over one billion people transformed itself into the megaglobal powerhouse Belt and Road Initiative, also known as the Silk Road Economic Belt and the twenty-first-century Maritime Silk Road development strategy, proposed by China's paramount leader Xi Jinping, which focuses on connectivity and cooperation between Eurasian countries, primarily the People's Republic of China (PRC), the land-based Silk Road Economic Belt (SREB), and the oceanic Maritime Silk Road (MSR).

The strategy underlines China's push to take a larger role in global affairs with a China-centered trading network.

In the past few years, the focuses were mainly on infrastructure investment, construction materials, railway and highway, automobile, real estate, power grid, and iron and steel.

However, while China spent the better part of the past fifty years as a relatively closed society, it has now recently flowered to bloom and is now actively engaging with the West as well as with Africa and South America to expand its influence and engage in project finance and loans, flush with billions in cash, ready to take on the world.

Ironically, the United States is going in the opposite trajectory, adopting a more protectionist and closed-off society, like Britain's Brexit phenomenon, after having spent the past fifty years openly engaging with the world, but now retreating into the shadows of America-first philosophy, focusing on taking control of its own economy and people.

This of course is paving the way for a Chinese-dominated global society, which can be both good and bad for global society.

Even though the Chinese are poised to take on the world as its economic global leader, there are still many things that they can learn from the United States:

(1) the rule of law;
(2) checks and balances within government;
(3) an end to dynastic wealth transfer and uber-oligarchy society;
(4) tolerance of different races, religions, viewpoints, and creeds;
(5) independence in starting and building business;

(6)   healthy skepticism of government; and

(7)   the spirit of ingenuity and invention.

China can also learn a great deal from America when it comes to placing human rights and civil liberties at the forefront of their culture, but this can also prove to be disastrous as Americans are currently experiencing a distinct balkanization of its people hitherto never seen before, with different factions of society at each other's throats on a seemingly endless and daily basis— blacks versus whites, women versus men, gays versus straight, Muslims versus Jews versus Christians, and other myriad social problems such as epidemic opioid addiction, breakdown of the nuclear family, sexually transmitted disease, and wide scale poverty.

Things aren't helped when it seems that the rich newly emerging oligarchs in America seem to be actively fomenting and funding America's recently visible deep fractures in society on behalf of their foreign brethren in international high-level business and banking.

This was the major reason China closed itself off in the first place, healing itself and licking its chops after the colonial plundering of its wealth and society by the Europeans, British, Japanese, Germans, Russians, French, and Portuguese.

China continued to be divided up into these spheres until the United States, which had no sphere of influence, grew alarmed at the possibility of its businessmen being excluded from Chinese markets.

In 1899, Secretary of State John Hay asked the major powers to agree to a policy of equal trading privileges. In 1900, several powers agreed to the US- backed scheme, giving rise to the Open Door policy, denoting freedom of commercial access and nonannexation of Chinese territory. In any event, it was in the European powers' interest to have a weak but independent Chinese government. The privileges of the Europeans in China were guaranteed in the form of treaties with the Qing government. In the event that the Qing government totally collapsed, each power risked losing the privileges that it already had negotiated.

The erosion of Chinese sovereignty and seizures of land from Chinese by foreigners contributed to a spectacular antiforeign outbreak rebellion in June 1900, when the Boxers (the society of righteous and harmonious fists) attacked foreigners around Beijing. The Imperial Court was divided into antiforeign and proforeign factions.

Extraterritorial jurisdiction was abandoned by the United Kingdom and the United States in 1943. Chiang Kai-shek forced the French to hand over all their concessions back to China control after World War II. Foreign political control over leased parts of China ended with the incorporation of Hong Kong and the small Portuguese territory of Macau into the People's Republic of China in 1997 and 1999 respectively.

China then closed off behind its Communist Iron Curtain, and the rest is history.

America's preoccupation and entanglement in foreign wars and the idiotic self-defeating war on terrorism after September 11, 2001, exhausted both its economy and its people, until the clamor grew so loud that the people began to rebel and demanded that its doors be closed to immigration and foreign entanglements.

Enter President Donald Trump who rose to power based on these American sentiments demanding that the doors be closed and that focus be paid to its own people and societal problems.

Now with the recent meeting by and between Presidents Donald Trump and Xi Jinping in November 2017, no starker contrast could be shown, and the roles of both super global powers have been dramatically reversed, one side protectionist and cautious (United States) and the other engaged and poised to take on the world (China).

However, just like China can learn from the United States, the exact opposite is also true. America can also greatly learn from China in the following:

(1) focusing on educating its people and encouraging study, rather than just having fun drinking, doing drugs, and having promiscuous sex without respite;

(2) encouraging strong family values and the nuclear family unit, as this fosters stronger, more balanced children and citizens, while warding away dependency on the state;

(3) curtailing organized and systemic corruption by jailing and punishing those business and government leaders who enrich themselves and their coffers at the expense of the populace;

(4) limiting addictions to social media, mindless video games, and brain rotting entertainment fanfare;

(5) zero tolerance policy for addictions of any kind;

(6) encouraging hard, industrious work and focus on the self and family;

(7) avoiding stupid foreign wars, colonial behavior, and entanglements with other nations' internecine conflicts and policies, and focusing on building and strengthening the nation itself;

(8) encouraging and fostering responsible mature behavior, rather than abject and self-destructive social stupidity;

(9) patriotism and love of country above all else.

It is important that China and the USA meet somewhere in the middle and learn to cross-pollinate to cooperate with one another and lead the inevitable global community into the future, supporting and encouraging each other as they go, without encroaching on or offending each other as time passes down through the centuries.

Social Media Time Usage Should Be Limited Either by Parents or Government

As long as this country is on a national security and emergency kick regulating the enormously damaging and debilitating use of illegal (and legal) opioids by the American masses, so too should this country have a come-to-Jesus moment about the incredibly harmful, addictive, socially disruptive, and mentally emotionally/psychologically destructive addiction that the American people (especially by its youth and the millennial generation, ages twenty to thirty-five) have with social media use and proliferation.

There is no longer any question that excessive addiction to, and use of, the countless social media applications (most popular are Facebook, Snapchat, Instagram, and yes, even Twitter) are stealing tens of billions of hours from productive activity such as work, exercise, study, time with friends and family, as well as other healthy social behavior patterns tending to make a human being a balanced, healthy individual.

Additionally, the incredibly harmful effect on the youth and young people in society are also being attacked by excessive social media usage and addiction when people are forced to portray themselves as equally, if not more, wealthy, glamorous, exciting, and interesting than the tens of millions of people in their social media circles, and this also leads to easily diagnosable and clinically proven feelings of insecurity, anxiety, low self-esteem, low self-worth, clinical depression, obesity, and desperation to achieve false, if not impossible, standards that do not really exist, and other psycho and sociosomatic mental illnesses.

Indeed, dishonest and evil social media professionals, application sites, and companies have been exposed and outed using different psychological techniques and mechanisms, much like the cigarette, alcohol, or drug industry, to lure and trap young people and others into dangerously addictive behaviors thereon, as was articulated in "Your Addiction to Social Media Is No Accident" by Julian Morgans.

Countless scientific studies have definitively proven and linked excessive social media use to failed or broken relationships with friends/family, failures in school or work performance, mental/physical/emotional breakdowns necessitating prescription (or illegal) drug/narcotics/opioid use and addiction, prostitution and dangerous sexual promiscuity, obesity, cheating and philandering in relationships, breakdowns in the family unit, loss of privacy and identity theft, robberies and violent crime, corporate and government espionage and unlawful surveillance, and even acts of suicide due to cyberbullying and online intimidation/defamation/slander/libel.

See for example Fox, J., & Rooney, M. C. (2015), "The Dark Triad and Trait Self-Objectification As Predictors of Men's Use And Self-presentation Behaviors on Social Networking Sites," *Personality & Individual Differences*, 76, 161–165, or Mehdizadeh, S. (2010), "Self-Presentation 2.0: Narcissism and Self-Esteem on Facebook," *Cyberpsychology, Behavior, and Social Networking*, 357–364.

In short, although the use of, exploration, and connecting online through social media is a reality in the modern-day American (and global) society, there can no longer be any doubt that excessive social media addiction is costing the United States trillions of dollars per year in unnecessary costs pertaining to health care, maintenance of children and salvage of the family unit, lawsuits, crime prevention and investigation, identity theft and loss of privacy, drug addiction, school and workplace lack of productivity, and other massive losses.

To that end, parents need to exercise more limitations on their dependent children's use of social media thereof, or the US government needs to establish reasonable limitations thereto, possibly based on taxation or cost issues when they exceed a certain congressionally determined amount of total time spent. This would require holding lengthy and thorough Congressional and Senate investigative hearings thereon, attended and participated in by social media experts, psychologists, health care professionals, law enforcement, employers, family law professionals, educational facilities, and others who could shed light and useful empirical data and information on the fiscal, as well as social, damages caused by the excessive use of, and addiction to, the phenomenon of social media.

Although the First Amendment to the United States Constitution theoretically allows unfettered use of social media and expression within the purview of freedom of speech, privacy, and other social communication mechanisms, the US government also has the power (and responsibility) to regulate or investigate, if any, exercise of this freedom impinges on, or drastically affects, national security, economy, safety, or health of the citizenry.

It is now time to at least look into this before it gets even worse.

Deep State Mandatory Arbitration Clauses Subvert the American People's Right to Sue

C leverly tucked away in almost each and every contract struck by and between the American people and the corporate/banking behemoths dotting the American landscape is a little-known (or understood) paragraph (or series of paragraphs) entitled mandatory arbitration clause.

Normally, 90 percent of people that enter into an online or corporate contract for services never really read in-depth these boring, verbose, horrifically complex little legalese arbitration clauses containing run-on sentences, dry grammar, and silly pronouns, which essentially sign away on these people's entire livelihoods, bank accounts, real property, money, human rights, civil liberties, constitutional guarantees, or even personal dignity.

And the worst part of all this is that the only ones who benefit from these arbitration clauses are the Deep State oligarchs who literally control, and are in the process of controlling even more, of the entire economic, technological, and financial marketplace, of virtually everything.

While more and more corporate/banking/technological behemoths are steadily moving toward more and more mergers and acquisitions, aided and abetted by an equally corrupt and cronied Federal Trade Commission (FTC) run by the same Deep State bastards for the last thirty years, buying one another out and further consolidating their own money and power at the expense of the American people, they are also increasingly and uniformly inserting a de rigueur arbitration clause demanding that the American masses and consumers that they do business with forever and absolutely relinquish and give up their right to sue or seek judicial or court redress for acts that federal case law has now clearly stated includes outright theft, deceit, racial or sexual or religious discrimination, verbal or physical abuse, dishonesty, unfairly targeting anyone based on anything that the corporate/banking CEO hates, and other outrageous and inhumane reasons that the founding fathers frankly fought a war with England to get away from.

The slow-motion recapturing of the American people and their property by the global oligarch banks and corporations is occurring right before the eyes of American patriots every single day—without the firing of a single shot.

The slow, painful, clandestine, and surreptitious subversion of the basic human rights, civil liberties, and constitutional protections that used to make the United States of America special are now rapidly going the way of the extinct dodo bird and are now becoming mere quaint and fond memories of an older generation of Americans, who can still remember that they could always sue whenever they were royally screwed over by a corporate/banking entity in any capacity.

Now, both state and federal judges, upon seeing a motion to compel arbitration submitted by a well-heeled, smug big law corporate attorney with really nice shoes and a five-thousand-dollar suit will noticeably shift uncomfortably in his seat (if he is honest) even when he is confronted with a complaint from a litigant that contains the most awful, mind-shattering, specific, backed-by-evidence, horrific, unethical, illegal, and human rights violating acts by that corporate/banking entity or its employees, because that judge knows fully well that there is absolutely no escape from that arbitration clause, and he must dismiss that case without bringing those perpetrators to justice, or letting a hearing continue, or even bringing them and their acts to light with discovery, because he could literally lose his job as a judge or be sanctioned/disciplined if he doesn't.

The arbitration tribunal where the injured complainant is inevitably shunted into, like a horse waiting to be shot, is invariably staffed by corporate/banking cronies of those criminal oligarchs who run those offending companies, and they all play golf or drink at the same country clubs together and are more in bed with one another than anyone truly realizes.

To add insult to injury, the aggrieved litigant must literally pay through the nose to take part in said arbitration, often going bankrupt in the process, only to literally get reamed out even further by that offending company's buddies on the arbitration panel.

This is truly the most sickening part of all this and desperately needs attention by the United States Congress and Senate to change/amend the laws governing mandatory arbitration clauses, but judging by the recent Republican gutting of the Consumer Financial Protection Bureau (CFPB) recently a few weeks ago, and the oligarch/plutocrat stranglehold on the banking/corporate entities in America (and the globe), this legislative investigation, review, amendment, and desperately needed change is not likely to happen anytime soon.

In fact, it is more likely to get worse, until the American people are all truly back as colonial subjects of England, where peasants were thrown into the stocks if they so much as offended the queen or her noblemen and favored subjects.

The situation in the judiciary with these mandatory arbitration clauses is truly dire and cries out for intervention, urgently, and immediately, by the United States Congress and Senate.

The Three Indians of the Apocalypse

For the better part of the last few hundred years, the most famous and celebrated individuals who managed to emerge from the Indian subcontinent have generally created great Karmic currency for their country and the world, through their mass exporting and transformation of the Western world with novel ideas such as nonviolence, civil disobedience, ahimsa, vegetarianism, yoga, meditation, spirituality, nonmaterialism, political neutrality, religious diversity/tolerance/pluralism, secularism, and other wonderful gifts bestowed on humanity by such internationally recognized luminaries such as Mahatma Gandhi, Jawaharlal Nehru, Swami Vivekananda, Subhash Chandra Bose, Indira Gandhi, Sai Baba, Dayananda Saraswati, Jiddu Krishnamurti, and scores of others, too numerous to even count.

It was said that venerated African American civil rights leader Rev. Martin Luther King Jr. was even influenced by the teachings of Mahatma Gandhi's teachings of nonviolence and civil disobedience, which led to the liberation of African Americans from the yoke of institutional racism and discrimination in the United States of America, and directly to the enactment of the Civil Rights Act of 1964, as well as attracting the Beatles and many millions of others who were drawn to the peaceful teachings and spirituality of classical Indian culture and civilization and its emissaries.

So what happened?

Within the past year alone, the Deep State oligarchs have decided to successfully exploit, use, and spend this vast spiritual currency and credibility painstakingly and slowly amassed by the people and culture of India, by using three of the most diabolical, ambitious, and seemingly sociopathic individuals of Indian origin to literally catapult many of their bloodthirsty and ruthless global goals to reality that no one leader in the world even dared to touch, let alone affix their names (and racial identities) to.

1) North Carolina Republican Governor Nikki Haley (real name Namrata Randawa) has seemingly sold her soul to continue to stoke war and provocation all around the world, especially with Russia, North Korea, and Iran, at the behest of the Deep State global oligarchs, as well as stoking bitter global fires and wars with Islam and Christianity when she pushed President Donald Trump to officially declare Jerusalem the capital of Israel and other war crimes and human rights violations too numerous to describe here.

2) FCC Republican Chairman Ajit Pai has single-handedly destroyed the internet by presiding over, and then repealing, the concept of net neutrality, which will cause the already monopolized different internet service providers to be able to pick and choose and block any and all internet content that they don't want the masses to read or see, at the behest of his massive telecommunications paymasters, with the people of America and the world to be damned.

3) Narendra Modi, Prime Minister of India, has completely demonetized that country, abruptly stealing/seizing any and all currencies from the poor and middle class in order to give it to the global oligarchs, who will use it to back up their fledgling property and assets, thus stripping the most vulnerable of his own people of their wealth, while giving it to the rich. Millions of people have either died, starved, or lost their businesses and homes because of this calamity, as well as tanked the once vibrant Indian economy which was growing at more than 7 percent each year for the past few decades, all at the behest and orders of his Deep State global oligarch masters.

Again, not one person in the world wanted to take the credit for any one of these horrific violent movements toward global unipolarity and slavery, but these three shortsighted sociopathic Indian-origin idiots did.

They have humiliated and robbed more than one billion of their fellow Indian origin people all over the world of the international goodwill that they previously enjoyed as described above and have reduced the Indian sociopolitical image and reputation to ashes, all in less than one year.

Each one of their assigned global developments is so extreme, so dire, that the world will forever be changed and has catapulted the planet even further toward cruel global oligarchy devoid of human rights and civil liberties, and ever closer to outright planetary feudalism and slavery.

These three miserable people of Indian origin have literally presided over and have been used by, the Deep State global oligarchs to pass laws and implement actions that are so severe, not even one single person in the world wanted to even touch or take the blame for it.

These three have also squandered and spent a great deal of the international good will that Indians have enjoyed and acquired over many centuries, specifically at the United Nations, global culture and consciousness, humanity, spirituality, and democracy.

Hopefully there will not be any more of these Indian-origin global prostitutes, who function and act like puppet marionettes at the behest of their global Deep State paymasters, for their own personal greed and avarice, as well as their selfish political ambitions.

Is MEK/Jundullah The ISIS Of Tomorrow

One would think that the United States would have learned by now, that it is never a good idea to arm terrorist groups in different parts of the world, due to the inevitable "blowback" which eventually ensues after these violent groups determine that the USA is no longer in support of them, or when the USA wants to deny that they have any relationship with them.

We have seen this paradigm unfold countless times before, over the past few decades, with groups like Al Qaeda, Al Nusra, La Fenice, Avanguardia Nazionale, Ordine Nuovo, the Contras, Cuban Exiles, Colombian Paramilitary Organizations, Los Pepes, Kosovo Liberation Army, Jundullah, Mujahedin-e Khalq ("MEK"), and countless others designed to engage in United States sponsored terrorist activities against sovereign governments and nations that the US doesn't like for whatever reason.

In the wake of the abject failure of the US using ISIS to destabilize, disrupt and disorient various governments throughout the Middle East, such as Syria, Iraq, Lybia, Yemen and others, followed quickly by various ISIS-attributed terrorist attacks against the US and Europe by ISIS, President Donald Trump was swept into office in large part because the American and European people discovered this via the veritable "sieve" known as social media and the internet.

But rather than change US foreign policy to ban or cease' using violent thugs to carry out US policy overseas, instead it appears that the US Government through the CIA have now adopted a smaller more surgically precise approach by supporting, through its proxy nations Israel and Saudi Arabia, smaller groups such as MEK and Jundullah, who operate primarily in tiny regions of the world, such as in and around Iran, without much of a global presence.

But like cancer, these groups have a tendency to grow uncontrollably, and then later turn on the US and Europe, when and if the latter starts to pull funding or divorce themselves from the court of public opinion through plausible denial.

This is exactly how ISIS grew into a formidable fighting force, and eventually turned on its creators, much like the Frankenstein monster in the Mary Shelley novels.

All of this must be an abject nightmare for the US FBI, DHS, ICE and DEA pull their proverbial hair out, because they must often clean up/explain the horrific domestic messes of terrorist blowback occurring on US soil when these groups inevitably turn on their paymasters, just like they are the chief law enforcement/preventative bodies that deal with the drug war, also in large part caused by the CIA's open and clandestine support of massive drug producing/trafficking regimes in Afghanistan, Colombia, Venezuela and Mexico.

The news lately has revealed that the US, Israel, and Saudi Arabia are openly funding, supporting, arming, training and providing logistical support to Jundullah and MEK in order to take down the current sovereign government of Iran.

Even though the USA, Saudi Arabia and Israel may not like the current government there, what right do they have to engage in this type of state sponsored terrorist behavior?

There is a reason why various governments throughout the world have stood the test of time, and exist in their present states.

Perhaps their people wanted it, or perhaps there was need for that specific type of ideology or mode of governance, but unless and until those governments actively target or harm Americans, the US has absolutely no business getting involved with those groups, and indeed, has invariably and inevitably lived to regret it countless times, in nearly 100% of all cases.

Extremism Has No Place In Political Discourse

The world's leaders have as of recently begun escalating a war of words with fiery rhetoric - but none of them can claim that they have the ultimate moral authority on everything.

While certain groups like to claim that the "other side" is the harbinger of hatred, evil and discrimination, that "target" almost always has an equally powerful and countervailing viewpoint, backed up by hundreds of millions of people.

The point being that, in this day and age of nuclear cataclysm, the world's leaders (global and local) no longer have the option of using fiery, divisive rhetoric to justify their political, and constituents' aims.

While this type of loud nonsense worked well for pre-modern day demagogues like Hitler, Mussolini, Stalin, Kruschev, and others, today in the modern age where 8 billion can communicate in real-time using the internet and social media, it is downright dangerous, misguided and stupid.

There are no more "good guys" and "bad guys," no more "boogeymen" hiding under the bed, only hundreds of millions of people at polar opposites of the political spectrum who will all die if their elected (and unelected) leaders succeed at irresponsibly baiting the nuclear beast.

Today's leaders must take stock, and take a step back, and realize that their first and chief order of business should be, not to kill all of their own people.

This means that fiery provocative rhetoric, no matter how angry or indignant or cornered that they feel, simply does not do anything but bring the world closer to nuclear annihilation.

And while certain segments of the global population automatically assume that their constituent base is the "end all, be all" viewpoint as to how the world should work, the fact remains that no one, no race, no religion, no ethnicity, no creed, no political viewpoint has the ultimate solution or answer to the problems facing the world today (if they did, their opponents would not exist today, due to the evolutionary process of natural selection).

The recent world news is rife with political, divisive rhetoric, from all sides of the religious, political, ethnic, racial, and identity politics spectrum, all for their own political benefit.

So while this past week, many of the world's people were upset with President Donald Trump's "shithole" comment, other parts of the world's people were equally upset with Democratic Congressman Luis Gutierrez' equally idiotic and offensive comment that Trump was some type of "Neo-Nazi" or "KKK" leader.

This type of "tennis-like" analysis can go back, and stretch the lines of time, all around the world, to the earliest days of human existence, with "tit for tat" comments and statements with no better etiology than the "chicken and egg" archetype - which came first, and who started this verbal exchange/diatribe?

Unfortunately since the dawn of time, the world's most well-funded and political masters of the universe, the global oligarchs, have always used this "us and them" type of dichotomy, using their "useful idiots" strategically placed within governments all around the world, for their own selfish "divide and conquer" strategies, only to further enrich their own pockets and consolidate and strengthen their own power, at the expense of eradicating and exterminating the world's, and their own, people.

So for minorities to accuse majorities, or majorities to accuse minorities, is both irrelevant and sad, because there are no longer any "minorities" or "majorities" anymore, just interlinked factions all across the globe, each in the hundreds of millions of souls.

To that end, before a leader, any leader, speaks, the first order of business should be: "who is this statement going to offend, and what are the consequences?"

Combating The Deep State Online

Now that President Donald Trump has declared an outright and open war on international terrorism all around the world, joining forces with Russian President Putin and Chinese Premier Xi, and scores of other world leaders to combat this enemy of civilization, in order to absolutely decimate violent actors around the planet who use destructive and disruptive means and methods other than political discourse to settle their differences, so too must he begin to now do, with regards to internet terrorism, slander, libel, defamation, terrorist threats, incitement to violence, and targeted harassment online.

As President Trump knows only too well, as he is a prime target of the Deep State/Oligarch/Global Terrorist Network online, with their relentless attacks on him, his wife, his family and his administration, when he developed the term "Fake News," he is also the only one who can finally find the balance between the U.S. Constitution First Amendment and terrorism carried out online.

Trump has repeatedly promised to "look at the libel laws," but what he should specifically look at is how to hold websites, their hosts, and their advertisers responsible and liable for their egregious taking advantage of the broad based immunities and protections afforded by the Communications Decency Act of 1996 Section 230 (aka "CDA 230"), drafted and passed by U.S. legislators such as Ron Wyden and Christopher Cox, which literally opened the floodgates to trillions of dollars of damage to individuals, small and large business, domestic and global relationships, national security, and global cohesion.

True enough, freedom of speech is paramount, and essential to the American constitutional experiment - but after 20 years of this "wild west" of internet speech, we know and have learned many things.

Various organized criminal enterprises have sprung up all over the world, extorting and blackmailing innocent people and businesses to pay them exorbitant amounts of money to remove/challenge anonymous, cowardly, false, defamatory, slanderous, libelous, terroristic, and incitement to violent threats online, always hiding behind the immunity and protection afforded by CDA 230 to both their own mafia-like "reputation management" websites, their web hosts, and their advertisers.

Much has also been revealed about the "ties" by and between these "reputation management" websites, and the offending websites themselves, so that if one pays one of these extortionate websites for "arbitration" or "challenging offending posts," one will suddenly find a dramatic increase in the exact same or similar postings on other offending websites, thus increasing damages, exposure, and of course, the "costs" attendant to getting these offensive and threatening posts off of the internet.

This is a classic racketeering enterprise, and each and every country has their own rules and laws governing such type of criminal activity, and in the United States, the most lax and forgiving of all of these types of crimes, it is called "RICO," or the Racketeering Influenced Corrupt Organization act.

This RICO law is a United States federal law that provides for extended criminal penalties and a civil cause of action for acts performed as part of an ongoing criminal organization.

The RICO Act focuses specifically on racketeering, and it allows the leaders of a syndicate to be tried for the crimes which they ordered others to do or assisted them in doing, closing a perceived loophole that allowed a person who instructed someone else to, to be exempt from the trial because they did not actually commit the crime personally.

Under RICO, a person who has committed "at least two acts of racketeering activity" drawn from a list of 35 crimes - 27 federal crimes and 8 state crimes within a 10 year period can be charged with racketeering if such acts are related to an "enterprise."

Those found guilty of racketeering can be fined up to $25,000 and sentenced to 20 years in prison per racketeering count.

In addition, the racketeer must forfeit all ill-gotten gains and interest in any business gained through a pattern of "racketeering activity."

This statute could easily be used against most of the "reputation management" websites which, like the Mafia, literally aid and abet, if not

"create" the online internet threats, targeting, harassment, incitement to violence, and terrorist threats in order to then charge a hefty "fee" to either "eradicate" or "combat" those self-created threats.

Indeed many business, banking, financial, communication, personal, and professional relationships can easily be discovered by and between these "reputation management" organized crime websites, and the other "offending websites" containing such illegal and unethical content.

The problem is that since at least 1996, the "Deep State" has successfully used the protections afforded by the CDA 230 to target their enemies online, discrediting and hobbling them at will, while simultaneously being able to weather the proverbial storm against themselves, because they are directly connected to the international central bankers with unlimited amounts of cash to survive personal or professional online destruction, while their targeted Deep State enemies are, by definition, "swimming upstream" against them, struggling barely to survive.

This is by no means a fair fight, and hundreds of millions of "dead" businesses and individuals have washed up on the shore in their wake, while Deep State connected individuals and businesses always seem to stay afloat.

So if President Donald Trump, arguably the greatest victim of the above referenced type of global online criminal activity on behalf of the Deep State, which is still relentlessly trying to destroy him, his family, his administration and his legacy, as well as average American individuals and businesses that he professes to care so much about, and if he is truly serious about "looking at the libel laws" as he has repeatedly stated/promised, then perhaps this is the best place for him to start.

About the Author

Wall Street attorney Rahul Manchanda shot to instant fame soon after he started his law practice in 2002, less than six months after the September 11, 2001, attacks.

Opening his law office only a few blocks away from ground zero, Mr. Manchanda became acutely aware of the massive changes that were coming down the pike for the United States of America and its people.

The transformation of the USA from a constitutional republic into a full-blown, oligarch-dominated fascist state seemed to be unstoppable and inevitable.

But Mr. Manchanda, assisted and supported by scores of freedom-loving, constitution-abiding, and patriotic colleagues, friends, and writers, began to expose this transmogrification of America into a country that none of the founding fathers would have recognized.

Voted as best lawyer repeatedly throughout his career, by scores of luminary attorney rating agencies and peer groups over and over throughout his twenty-year career in law, Attorney Rahul Manchanda has appeared countless times in the mainstream media on television and print and then switched gears to become a pioneer and visionary in the alternative media outlets when it seemed that the mainstream media was co-opted by the global oligarch money powers that be in order to fuel and brainwash the American and world's people into going along with their bloodthirsty and ruthless agenda.

Mr. Manchanda lives in Manhattan but frequently travels throughout the world to experience firsthand the different views and cultures of the people that inhabit it.